'On the base of the Pillar was a white poster. Gathered around were groups of men and women. Some looked at it with serious faces, others laughed and sniggered. I began to read it with a smile, but my smile ceased as I read. Clarke I had known through a friend of ours, Major MacBride, who used to come across the city to buy cigars in his little shop. Pearse I had seen for the first time a few minutes before. A man in the crowd had shouted out his name as a quiet-faced figure in uniform with a strange, green, soft hat had passed slowly out through the front door of the GPO. He had talked with an officer underneath the portico beside a fluted pillar. His face was firm and composed. Connolly I had heard speak at meetings. I had seen MacDonagh in the university where he had lectured on English, gayer than the other lectures. Plunkett was editor of *The Irish Review,* back numbers of which I had read. They did not mean anything – only names. As I stood looking at the GPO, pigeons fluttered up from the roof and with flat dives flew swiftly in different directions ...'

ERNIE O'MALLEY *ON ANOTHER MAN'S WOUND*

The General Post Office

Contents

Illustrations

ACKNOWLEDGEMENTS

The author and publisher wish to thank the following who have kindly given permission to reproduce photographs on the pages listed. Kilmainham Gaol and Museum: pp.21, 35, 36, 39, 48, 62, 65, 87; National Library of Ireland: pp. 8, 9, 25, 68, 78, 85; National Museum of Ireland: p. 20.

THE SEVEN
SIGNATORIES
OF THE
PROCLAMATION
OF THE
IRISH REPUBLIC
EASTER 1916

P.H. Pearse

Thomas J. Clarke

James Connolly

Thomas MacDonagh

Sean MacDiarmada

Eamonn Ceannt

Joseph Plunkett

THE PROCLAMATION OF

POBLACHT NA H EIREANN.

THE PROVISIONAL GOVERNMENT
OF THE

IRISH REPUBLIC
TO THE PEOPLE OF IRELAND.

IRISHMEN AND IRISHWOMEN: In the name of God and of the dead generations from which she receives her old tradition of nationhood, Ireland, through us, summons her children to her flag and strikes for her freedom.

Having organised and trained her manhood through her secret revolutionary organisation, the Irish Republican Brotherhood, and through her open military organisations, the Irish Volunteers and the Irish Citizen Army, having patiently perfected her discipline, having resolutely waited for the right moment to reveal itself, she now seizes that moment, and, supported by her exiled children in America and by gallant allies in Europe, but relying in the first on her own strength, she strikes in full confidence of victory.

We declare the right of the people of Ireland to the ownership of Ireland, and to the unfettered control of Irish destinies, to be sovereign and indefeasible. The long usurpation of that right by a foreign people and government has not extinguished the right, nor can it ever be extinguished except by the destruction of the Irish people. In every generation the Irish people have asserted their right to national freedom and sovereignty; six times during the past three hundred years they have asserted it in arms. Standing on that fundamental right and again asserting it in arms in the face of the world, we hereby proclaim the Irish Republic as a Sovereign Independent State, and we pledge our lives and the lives of our comrades-in-arms to the cause of its freedom, of its welfare, and of its exaltation among the nations.

The Irish Republic is entitled to, and hereby claims, the allegiance of every Irishman and Irishwoman. The Republic guarantees religious and civil liberty, equal rights and equal opportunities to all its citizens, and declares its resolve to pursue the happiness and prosperity of the whole nation and of all its parts, cherishing all the children of the nation equally, and oblivious of the differences carefully fostered by an alien government, which have divided a minority from the majority in the past.

Until our arms have brought the opportune moment for the establishment of a permanent National Government, representative of the whole people of Ireland and elected by the suffrages of all her men and women, the Provisional Government, hereby constituted, will administer the civil and military affairs of the Republic in trust for the people.

We place the cause of the Irish Republic under the protection of the Most High God, Whose blessing we invoke upon our arms, and we pray that no one who serves that cause will dishonour it by cowardice, inhumanity, or rapine. In this supreme hour the Irish nation must, by its valour and discipline and by the readiness of its children to sacrifice themselves for the common good, prove itself worthy of the august destiny to which it is called.

Signed on Behalf of the Provisional Government,

THOMAS J. CLARKE,

SEAN Mac DIARMADA,   THOMAS MacDONAGH,

P. H. PEARSE,   EAMONN CEANNT,

JAMES CONNOLLY.   JOSEPH PLUNKETT.

Introduction

The 1916 Proclamation is rightly regarded as a significant document in the history of Ireland and will forever remain a great historical landmark. It contains the first formal assertion of the Irish Republic as a sovereign independent state. And as well as being a proclamation of independence, it is also a declaration of rights. The signatories underlined their commitment to its ideals by pledging their own lives and the lives of their comrades-in-arms to the cause of the freedom of Ireland and the right of its people to a government of its own.

The Proclamation provided both the rationale and justification for the Rising of 1916 on historical and ethical grounds and set out the principles and values on which an Irish Republic should be created. As well as being inspired by Ireland's past, it was imbued with ideals which to this day exert a profound influence.

The principle of equality was enshrined in its opening words and expanded in paragraph four:

> The Republic guarantees religious and civil liberty, equal rights and equal opportunities to all its citizens, and declares its resolve to pursue the happiness and prosperity of the whole nation and of all its parts, cherishing all the children of the nation equally, and oblivious of the differences carefully fostered by an alien government, which have divided a minority from the majority in the past.

The Proclamation of the Republic did not of itself result in the establishment of a *de facto* republic – this had to await years of struggle – but it is a fact of history that its sovereignty was first proclaimed by the men of 1916 acting on behalf of the Irish people. And no other event in modern Irish history has been more significant in its results than the Proclamation of the Irish Republic on Easter Monday 1916.

The Proclamation concluded by praying that no one who served the cause of freedom 'will dishonour it by cowardice, inhumanity, or rapine. In this supreme hour the Irish nation must, by its valour and discipline ... prove itself worthy of the august destiny to which it is called.'

And so it turned out; the men fought gallantly and their adversaries admitted that they had observed all the rules of war, and no act of inhumanity, wantonness or terrorism had besmirched their cause.

This is a new edition of my publication of 1986, revised in the light of the further information that became available in 1991, as set out in chapter 4. In this connection I am indebted to the National Archives for permission to use the Memorandum of October 1953 to Eamon de Valera. For permission to use photographs I am grateful to Kilmainham Gaol and Museum, the National Library and the National Museum. The extracts from *Revolutionary Woman, An Autobiography*, and *On Another Man's Wound*, are courtesy of O'Brien Press, and Cormac O'Malley. I also appreciate the assistance and advice of Rena Dardis of Anvil Books.

JOHN O'CONNOR
September 1999

1 Background

The establishment of a free and independent Republic in Ireland had been the hope of Wolfe Tone and Robert Emmet. Other patriots down the years struggled for the ideal of separation and independence in one form or another. Republican separatism was the ultimate objective of the Irish Republican Brotherhood founded in 1858, which became popularly known as the Fenians. Though the IRB was a secret oath-bound society it was, in its early years, honeycombed with spies and its first attempt at armed revolt – the Fenian Rising of 1867 – proved abortive. However, the IRB lived on as an organisation and it always had its selected group ready to act as 'The Provisional Government of the Irish Republic'. It continued to have close associations with the Irish-American Clan na Gael.

Following the outbreak of the Great War in 1914, Clan na Gael proposed to the Supreme Council of the IRB in Ireland that a rebellion should be organised. It had long been a nationalist maxim that 'England's danger is Ireland's opportunity', so the Supreme Council agreed that Ireland should take advantage of England's involvement in the war and decided that another armed attempt to overthrow British rule in Ireland and establish a republic should be made before the war ended. An inner IRB Military Council, separate from the Supreme Council, was set up to plan the Rising. In view of the lessons of history and to preserve absolute secrecy, the Military Council was comprised of only a selected few of the trusted leaders: Thomas J. Clarke, Padraig Pearse, Sean MacDiarmada, Joseph Plunkett and Eamonn Ceannt. In January 1916 Thomas MacDonagh and James Connolly became members, making seven members in all. These were the seven signatories of the Proclamation.

Four members of the Military Council – Pearse, Plunkett, Ceannt and MacDonagh – were also high-ranking officers and members of the eight-man Headquarters Executive of the Irish Volunteers, which had been developed into a well-trained and disciplined body since its foundation in 1913. The Military Council, aware that Eoin MacNeill, Chief of Staff, and other members of the Volunteers Executive did not favour a direct initiative in armed insurrection, preferring to adopt a wait-and-see defensive policy. In the circumstances the Military Council kept the Volunteers Executive in the dark as to its intentions. It had, however, secretly placed IRB men in positions of responsibility and authority in the hope of securing effective control of the Volunteers when the time came for the Rising.

The intensive planning and preparations for the Rising had been proceeding during 1915 in the greatest secrecy, and in January 1916 the Military Council decided on the date – Easter Sunday, 23 April 1916. In his capacity as Director of Operations, Pearse published an order in the *Irish Volunteer* of 8 April 1916, with the approval of Eoin MacNeill and the Volunteers Executive, for a general mobilisation and manoeuvres of all units of the Volunteers on Easter Sunday. This order was in furtherance of the Military Council's secret decision for the Rising, a fact which was not apparent at the time to MacNeill or the Volunteers Executive. The Rising was still a closely guarded secret, known only to the members of the Military Council and very few others – none of them connected with the Volunteers. Nevertheless there was an air of expectancy among the Volunteers that something big was afoot.

During Holy Week, the Military Council met to finalise plans for the Rising. A Provisional Government was constituted and the drafting of the historic Proclamation of the Irish Republic, calling on the Irish people for their allegiance to the new nation, was finalised. Each of the seven members of the Provisional Government who agreed the Proclamation took upon himself the responsibility for the Rising, whether it should succeed or fail. By common consent the honour of being the first signatory was given to the unrepentant Fenian, Thomas J. Clarke, who can truly be described as the vital inspirational force of the Rising. The others were Padraig Pearse, who was chosen as President of the Provisional Government, Sean MacDiarmada, Joseph Plunkett, James Connolly, Thomas MacDonagh and Eamonn Ceannt.

That same week was to see a series of unexpected and dramatic developments which almost resulted in the Rising not taking place at all.

In an effort to win MacNeill's co-operation, on the Tuesday of Holy Week he was led to believe that the British were contemplating taking direct action against the Volunteers and arresting their leaders. Therefore, on Wednesday, he issued an order to the Volunteers to resist and defend themselves. However, the following

THE BRITISH GOVERNMENT'S PLAN

. . . FOR . . .

SUPPRESSING THE IRISH VOLUNTEERS.

WHOLESALE ARRESTS AND MASSACRE DECIDED UPON.

ARCHBISHOP OF DUBLIN TO BE MADE PRISONER.

The following is a transcript of a secret document in cipher at present in Dublin Castle. It is made public by a High Official whose conscience revolted when he learned the details of the plot.

" The following measures have been sanctioned by the Irish Office on the recommendation of the General Officer Commanding the Forces in Ireland. All preparations will be made to put these measures in force immediately on receipt of an order issued from the Chief Secretary's Office, Dublin Castle, and signed by the Under Secretary and the General Officer Commanding the Forces in Ireland. First, the following persons to be placed under arrest :—All members of the Sinn Fein National Council ; the Central Executive Irish Sinn Fein Volunteers ; General Council Irish Sinn Fein Volunteers ; County Board Irish Sinn Fein Volunteer's ; Executive Committee National Volunteers ; Coisde Gnota Committee Gaelic League. See List (a) three and four and Supplementary List (a) two . . . .

. . . . . . Dublin Metropolitan Police and Royal Irish Constabulary Forces in Dublin City will be confined to barracks under direction of Competent Military Authority. An order will be issued to inhabitants of city to remain in their houses until such time as Competent Military Authority may otherwise direct or permit ; pickets chosen from units of territorial force will be placed at all points marked on maps three and four accompanying ; mounted patrols will continuously visit all points and report every hour. The following premises will be occupied by adequate forces and all necessary measures used without need of reference to headquarters :— First, premises known as Liberty Hall, Beresford Place ; number six Harcourt Street, Sinn Fein Building ; number two Dawson Street, Headquarters Volunteers ; number twelve D'Olier Street, *Nationality* Office ; number twenty-five Rutland Square, Gaelic League Office ; number forty-one Rutland Square, Foresters' Hall ; Sinn Fein Volunteer premises in city ; all National Volunteer premises in city ; Trade Council premises, Capel Street ; Surrey House, Leinster Road, Rathmines. The following premises will be isolated and all communication to or from prevented : Premises known as Archbishop's House, Drumcondra ; Mansion House, Dawson Street ; number forty Herbert Park ; Larkfield, Kimmage Road ; Woodtown Park, Ballyboden ; Saint Enda's College, Hermitage, Rathfarnham ; and in addition premises in List five (d). See Maps three and four."

NOTE :—The reader will observe that this dastardly plan provides for the imprisonment of the spiritual, civic, and industrial guides of the people—the Archbishop, the Mansion House, and the Trades Council are to be prevented from interfering whilst the massacre of the Volunteers by the Military is in progress.

*Eoin MacNeill
Chief of Staff of the
Volunteers*

day he found out that the rumours of impending British actions were not true; he also 'got wind of the word' that something more than parades and manoeuvres were intended for Easter Sunday.

MacNeill immediately went to see Pearse and insisted on being told the truth. He was told, for the first time, of the planned Rising. He was completely opposed to the action. On Good Friday, Pearse, MacDiarmada and MacDonagh again saw MacNeill and told him for the first time of the expected arrival of arms from Germany and apparently succeeded in persuading him that there was no alternative but to carry out their plans for the Rising. But, with the moves and countermoves, the situation was changing from hour to hour. News came through on Easter Saturday of the failure to land the German arms in Kerry, the loss of three Volunteers near

Killorglin – the first casualties of 1916 – on Good Friday night, and the arrest of Roger Casement. As Chief of Staff of the Volunteers, MacNeill issued a final countermanding order and had it published in the *Sunday Independent* on Easter Sunday 1916:

All orders given to Irish Volunteers for Easter Sunday are hereby rescinded and no parades, marches or other movements of Irish Volunteers will take place.

Though earlier in April the British Admiralty had decoded messages concerning the departure of the *Aud* carrying arms from Germany, Dublin Castle intelligence had no definite information about the planned Rising. But the authorities continued to watch developments closely and were in constant session with their military and police advisers during Holy Week. The reassuring news of the scuttling of the *Aud,* coupled with the countermanding order for Easter Sunday, led them to conclude that with these setbacks the immediate danger of an uprising could now be regarded as passed. However, the authorities, at meetings in Dublin Castle and the Vice-Regal Lodge, did seriously consider taking steps for the arrest of suspected leaders on Easter Sunday or Monday, as well as raiding Liberty Hall. Then it was decided to defer any such direct action until some days later.

In the meanwhile the Military Council was very active. The members were disappointed and dismayed at the turn of events but not discouraged. They met at Liberty Hall early on Easter Sunday and considered that they had no alternative but to accept that the countermanding of the manoeuvres on that day meant that the planned nationwide Rising could not now take place on that day. Their plans might have gone awry but it was unanimously decided by one o'clock to proceed with the plans already prepared for Dublin, which were not dependent on foreign aid. The words of Pearse, *'Do thugas m'aghaidh ar an ród seo romham'*, caught the mood of the men who took that fateful and historic decision:

> I have turned my face
> To this road before me
> To the deed that I see
> And the death I shall die.

Dublin Castle seriously underestimated the strength of mind and purpose of the leaders and were completely unaware of the moves of the Military Council on the vital days before the Rising. The authorities were afterwards held to blame for not forestalling the Rising by arresting the leaders.

By noon on Easter Monday the Rising had begun. Five of the signatories of the Proclamation were in the General Post Office in Dublin. Pearse, Connolly and Plunkett had marched from Liberty Hall at the head of a combined force of Volunteers and Citizen Army, met up with Clarke and MacDiarmada, and established the headquarters of the Provisional Government there. The first flag raised on the flag-staff at the corner of the GPO and Princes Street was a green flag bearing the inscription 'Irish Republic' in large Gaelic script. The tricolour flag of green, white and orange was hoisted soon after.

Shortly after noon, Padraig Pearse, standing beneath

the high portico of the GPO and flanked by his colleagues read the Proclamation publicly proclaiming Ireland a republic and a sovereign independent state, acknowledged or not, and the setting up of a Provisional Government.

Pearse concluded the reading of the Proclamation with the words: 'In this supreme hour the Irish nation must, by its valour and discipline and the readiness of its children to sacrifice themselves for the common good, prove itself worthy of the august destiny to which it is called.' As he did, James Connolly clasped his hand and cried out, 'Thanks be to God, Pearse, that we have lived to see this day.'

Footnote: The bullet-riddled green flag was confiscated after the Rising by the British forces. Attempts by the Irish Government to have it returned failed until the then British Labour Prime Minister, Harold Wilson, secretly gave the order in 1966 for its return to the reluctant curator of the Imperial War Museum. It is now in the safe-keeping of the National Museum in Dublin.

The green flag flown over the GPO during Easter Week.

ARMY OF THE IRISH REPUBLIC

(Dublin Command)

Headquarters

Date.. 24th April, 1916

To

Officer in Charge, Reis & D.B.C
Reis's

The main purpose of your post is to protect our wireless station. Its secondary purpose is to observe Lower Abbey Street and Lower O'Connell Street. Commandere in the D.B.C. whatever food and utensils you require. Make sure of a plentiful supply of water wherever your men are. Break all glass in the windows of the rooms occupied by you for fighting purpose. Establish a connection between your forces in the D.B.C. and in Reis's building. Be sure that the stairways leading immediately to your rooms are well barricaded. We have a post in the house at the corner Bachelor's Walk, in the Hotel Metropole, in the Imperial Hotel, in General Post Office. The directions from which you are likely to be attacked are from the Custom House, or from the far side of the river, Dolier Street or Westmoreland Street We believe there is a sniper in McBurneys on the far side of the river

James Connolly
Commandant General

SINN FEIN REVOLT.

Reproduction of Despatch, April, 1916.

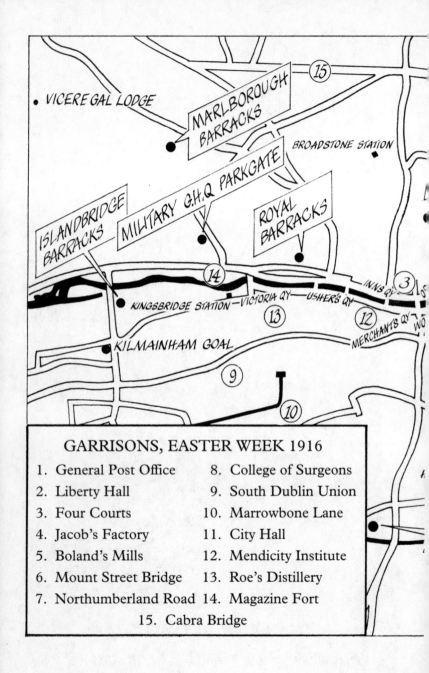

GARRISONS, EASTER WEEK 1916

1. General Post Office
2. Liberty Hall
3. Four Courts
4. Jacob's Factory
5. Boland's Mills
6. Mount Street Bridge
7. Northumberland Road
8. College of Surgeons
9. South Dublin Union
10. Marrowbone Lane
11. City Hall
12. Mendicity Institute
13. Roe's Distillery
14. Magazine Fort
15. Cabra Bridge

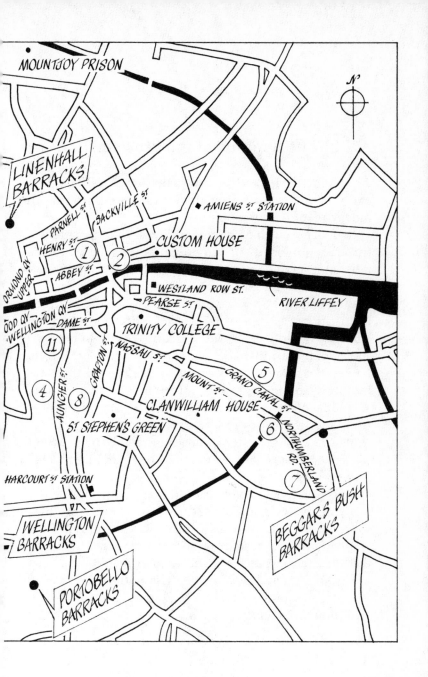

2 The Drafting of the Proclamation

An essential element of the plans for the Rising was the issue of a founding document proclaiming an independent Irish Republic.

It is believed that the actual literary composition of the Proclamation, in language expressive of ideals inherently heroic, is largely the work of Pearse, a view supported by the evidence of Kathleen Clarke in her autobiography *Revolutionary Woman*. When he returned from the crucial meeting of the Military Council on Tuesday of Holy Week, her husband Tom told her how the Proclamation had been drawn up: 'Some time before Pearse had been asked to draft it on the lines intimated to him and submit it to the Council. He did, and some changes were made.' An intriguing sidelight is that one of the seven thought equal opportunities should not be given to women but, tantalisingly, except for saying that Tom was not that one, she doesn't say who was.

The positive influence of James Connolly in the drafting is seen in its assertion of the claims of a sovereign people to social justice and the control of the country's natural resources. It is not certain what input the other five signatories had, but they would have been united in faith and pride in the Irish nation, the passion for freedom and social justice, and the ideal of a civilisation inherently Irish which had inspired Ireland's resistance to conquest for centuries.

The Irish Citizen Army outside Liberty Hall

The final version of the unanimously agreed Proclamation, consisting of two sheets of paper, was given
to Thomas MacDonagh for secret keeping. At the
meeting of the Military Council on Easter Sunday
morning in Liberty Hall, he handed it over to James
Connolly to whom had been assigned the responsibility
for having it printed.

3 The Printing of the Proclamation

The printing shop in Liberty Hall was located in a small room, 9 x 7 feet, and the only natural lighting came from a single window. In addition to the confined space, the facilities for printing were of a restricted nature and would have proved inadequate for the job of printing the Proclamation were it not for the resourcefulness of the men selected to do the typesetting and printing.

The machine to be used, an ancient model of a Double Crown Wharfdale, was in a rather run-down condition. It had been purchased by Connolly in 1915 when he found difficulty getting a printer willing to produce the *Workers' Republic* because of the inflammatory and seditious nature of its contents. Connolly had also arranged for a supply of type for this machine from a friendly printer, Joseph Stanley of Liffey Street. However, when members of the Citizen Army, dressed as ordinary workmen, arrived with a handcart to collect the type, they found that the police had raided the printing works and seized practically all the type. They had, however, overlooked a number of frames already set up. These were collected and taken to Liberty Hall. Though he had only a limited range of type and a not-very-satisfactory machine, Connolly nevertheless was able to print the *Workers' Republic* in Liberty Hall. Because rebel journals had been banned by the Government in 1914 he took the precaution of having an armed guard from the Citizen Army to protect his equipment.

Connolly at the time was acting General Secretary of the Irish Transport and General Workers' Union and was able to obtain the agreement of the executive of the union to these arrangements. Thus, there was in operation in Liberty Hall in 1915 a small resistance press which was not discovered until the Rising was well under way.

On Good Friday 1916 three men – Michael J. Molloy and Liam O Briain, compositors, and Christopher Brady, printer, who had been helping in the work of printing the *Workers' Republic* were secretly given notice by Connolly that they were to print the Proclamation on poster-size paper that he would provide. From their experience on the *Workers' Republic,* the men felt that there would not be enough type for a job of this size in the printing shop in Liberty Hall. But realising the all-important nature of the message to the Irish people that would be contained in the Proclamation, they set about finding solutions. One possibility was borrowing type from another source. Michael Molloy knew a printer in nearby Capel Street named William Henry West, an Englishman known to be a man of integrity and a rebel at heart, who had done an amount of printing for the independence movement and never seemed to care whether he was paid or not. Molloy went down to Capel Street and Mr West willingly gave him a fount of type consisting of a pair of cases for each of the two compositors, four cases of type in all, as well as handfuls of assorted type. This bounty was placed on a handcart pushed by a Citizen Army man named Andy Monahan (known as Dazzler) and taken to Liberty Hall. Thus it came about that the principal fount of type used in the printing of the Proclamation was supplied by an Englishman.

When Molloy, O Briain and Brady presented themselves for special duty on 9 o'clock on Easter Sunday morning they were placed under immediate arrest. The order for arrest was given by James Connolly to Captain William Partridge of the Citizen Army guard at Liberty Hall; the reason was to safeguard their interests in case the premises were stormed and raided, by enabling them to plead 'work under duress'. The police, aware that Liberty Hall was the hub of patriotic activities, had been keeping the premises under constant and close observation. They were there that Easter Sunday morning, as it had become known that the Volunteers had delivered a quantity of explosives. However, neither they nor the military authorities were prepared to risk an attack on Liberty Hall because of the knowledge that they would be met with armed resistance from the Citizen Army guard.

When the men set to work, the plan was to divide the work of composing by cutting the two sheets of the manuscript into four sections, each compositor selecting a number of paragraphs which he proceeded to set up by himself, using his own two cases of type. The work was at an advanced stage when it became obvious that neither man could complete his portion of the work because neither had sufficient type. Having consulted Connolly, a solution to this difficulty was soon found. Half the Proclamation would be printed and, when this had been done, the type used in the upper half would be freed and could be used for the lower half. Thus it was necessary to utilise the resources of the four cases of type for setting each section of the job, and the Proclamation had to be printed in two operations. Even at that, the men had to work until late on Easter Sunday night and Connolly had to be consulted on particular difficulties.

The upper part of the Proclamation, down to the words 'among the nations' at the end of the third paragraph, were the first to be set up. Over 1,000 copies were then printed off on the full-size poster paper. Connolly's original order was for 2,500 copies (if the Rising had been general throughout Ireland it had been the intention to supply the country as well as Dublin with copies) but there was not sufficient paper to print that quantity. After completing the printing of the upper part, the type was broken up and distributed and set up in the cases for the printing of the lower part, from 'The Irish Republic is entitled ...' at the beginning of the fourth paragraph to the end. This section was then printed off on the sheets already printed with the upper part.

As the printing was done in two sections, the space dividing the two sections is not always the same as can seen in the copies of the original Proclamation that have survived; if a proper printing machine had been available this would not have been the case. Another factor was the paper which, being of poor quality, was not always square. The Wharfdale proved troublesome and time-consuming in use and required the constant attention and mechanical expertise of Christopher Brady to keep it operating. He also found it impossible to achieve even inking of the type; the rollers refused to maintain an even pressure, with the result that there was much smudging in parts and faint printing in others. Typographically there were other difficulties; the line spaces were constantly forcing their way up and had repeatedly to be forced down again. Brady's feat in joining the two halves was not inconsiderable.

The heading 'POBLACHT NA H EIREANN' was printed in plain wooden type, all in full capitals, while the next lines, also in wooden letters, show an attempt to break the monotony by introducing ornamental lettering with bent arms and serifs.

THE PROCLAMATION OF

POBLACHT NA H EIREANN.

THE PROVISIONAL GOVERNMENT

OF THE

IRISH REPUBLIC

TO THE PEOPLE OF IRELAND.

The two lines, 'THE PROVISIONAL GOVERN-MENT' and 'TO THE PEOPLE OF IRELAND', contain six Os; two, in 'TO' and 'OF', are in the correct fount – the other four are plain non-serif type. The fifth line, 'IRISH REPUBLIC', also contains a wrong fount; the 'C' is a smaller type size and appears to be a converted 'O'.

A further curiosity occurs in line six, 'TO THE PEOPLE OF IRELAND'; the fount of type in this size was incomplete and the men ran short of the letter 'E' – an examination of the word 'THE' reveals that the 'E' is really an 'F' converted with some sealing-wax into a very tolerable 'E'.

In the main body of the Proclamation there is a wrong fount 't' in the word 'extinguished' in line 13. But it was with the letter 'e' that the compositors ran into real trouble. In all, the document contains 154 'e's'. Anyone who takes the trouble to count them will find that in the top section there are 131 correct or regular and 23 different or wrong 'e's'; in the lower half there are 109 correct and no wrong fount 'e's'.

In the first line of the final paragraph there is an inverted 'e' in the word 'the' before 'protection'. The word 'protection' appears to be 'proteetion' but that is not so; the 'c' is another example of dirty type and is so smudged as to appear like an 'e'.

The names of the seven signatories at the bottom of the Proclamation are all spelt correctly. The first name to appear on a line to itself is THOMAS J. CLARKE, while underneath, in two sloping columns, are the names of the others:

```
                THOMAS J. CLARKE,
SEAN Mac DIARMADA,      THOMAS MacDONAGH,
    P. H. PEARSE,            EAMONN CEANNT,
     JAMES CONNOLLY.         JOSEPH PLUNKETT.
```

There is a comma after each name except those of James Connolly and Joseph Plunkett, after which there are full stops. At first glance the 'M' in Eamonn Ceannt's name appears to be a converted 'N' but on close examination it turns out to be another example of smudging or filling in.

The paper used for the printing of the Proclamation was purchased by James Connolly from the Saggart Paper Mills in Dublin. It was in the nature of a bargain, being a cheap line of paper in poster size which the mills had in stock. It was similar to that usually used in the printing of the *Workers' Republic*. The colour might best be described as white with a greyish tinge through it; it was of poor quality as far as texture was concerned and so thin that it would quite easily tear. It could not survive for long in outdoor conditions – which partly explains the rarity of original copies of the Proclamation.

The work of printing was completed on Monday morning and the men, as instructed by Connolly, handed over the 1,000 copies to Captain William Partridge or Miss Helena Maloney, who had reported with the Citizen Army at Liberty Hall. They were then sent over to the GPO.

The Proclamation having been publicly read by Pearse, as President of the Provisional Government, Connolly detailed Sean T. O'Kelly to distribute copies throughout the centre of Dublin. Armed with a bucket of hastily made paste, the future President of Ireland, who afterwards whimsically described himself as 'bill-poster to the Republic', began an historic round of his native city. From Princes Street he emerged into O'Connell Street, pasting, as he went, copies on the pillars of the GPO, the plinths of statues, shop-fronts, even one on the gate post of Trinity College.

He had some copies left over and, with a fine sense of the historic importance of the occasion, he took steps to make sure some of them survived. With a nice ironic touch, he got three British Government official envelopes from the offices in the GPO and into each one he folded a copy of the Proclamation – one to Monsignor Curran, then Secretary to the Archbishop of Dublin, one to his fiancée, Phyllis Ryan, and the third to his mother. Realising that the GPO would be attacked during the hostilities, he posted them, not there, but in a post-box in a nearby street. Two of these envelopes were never delivered but the one addressed to his mother arrived safely a week after the Rising. The O'Kelly family kept this copy carefully all through the years. Today it hangs in its frame in a honoured place in Leinster House, home of the Dáil, the parliament of the Republic of Ireland, certified as follows: *Deimhniú gur buan cóip i seo den dhfógra a léig Pádraig Mac Piarais, Luan Cásca, 1916 – Seán T. Ó Ceallaigh.*

Another true original of the Proclamation, certified and authenticated as such by the men who printed it – Michael J. Molloy, Liam O Briain and Christopher Brady – is in the National Museum; on the back are the signatures of 1916 prisoners in Mountjoy, dated 19 May 1916. It was donated by Dr Kathleen Lynn who had been attached to Countess Markievicz's battalion at the St Stephen's Green post during the Rising. Other true originals can be seen in University College, Dublin (presented by Mr Colm O Lochlainn, also a participant in the Rising), and in the Library of Trinity College, Dublin (on loan from the Kilmainham Gaol Restoration Committee). The copy sent by Tom Clarke from the GPO on Easter Monday by special messenger to his wife was presented by her to the Kilmainham Gaol Museum.

It is believed that a copy of the Proclamation is in the possession of the British Government, probably filed away in their archives, but this cannot be confirmed. It is known that Lord Wimbourne, the then Lord Lieutenant, sent a despatch about the Rising to Prime Minister Asquith on Easter Tuesday, 25 April 1916, in which he stated that the insurgents had posted a Proclamation setting up a Provisional Republican Government throughout the city and he enclosed a copy of it. A copy was also used by the British authorities as evidence at the courts martial of the signatories.

Authentic copies of the Proclamation printed at Liberty Hall on Easter Sunday are rare and precious documents. A genuine copy can be recognised by the following criteria:

1 Size of paper – it should measure 20 x 30 inches (508 x 762 mm).
2 Type area should be 29 inches (736 mm) and length of line 18¹/₄ inches (463 mm).
3 Paper is a poor poster-type quality. Colour, white with a greyish tinge.
4 The spacing between the upper and lower sections of the Proclamation varies. In the copy in the National Museum it is ⁵/₈ of an inch (16 mm), whereas in the Leinster House copy it is ⁵/₁₆ of an inch (8 mm).
5 Typography includes different founts of type; various peculiarities have been described on pages 30–1.
6 Punctuation differs after the names of the signatories, and the 'M' in Eamonn Ceannt's name is smudged.
7 It is undated.

What became of the original manuscript? The pages from which the printers worked have, unfortunately, been lost forever. It is generally believed that they were left in Liberty Hall after the printing had been completed. The building was shattered by gunfire and shelling and swept by flames during the following week and thus one of Ireland's most historic documents disappeared.

Liberty Hall after the Rising

When the British Army entered the shelled Liberty Hall on Wednesday, 26 April, they discovered the old Wharfdale machine in the printing room, with the lower half of the Proclamation still intact in the machine. The printer's original intention had been to break up the type but owing to the lateness of the hour on Easter Monday morning when the printing was finished this was not done. The soldiers were puzzled about the whereabouts of the rest of the type and searched unavailingly for it, not knowing of course that the Proclamation had been printed in two halves. They then proceeded to run off copies of this lower half as souvenirs and distributed some to friends and sightseers

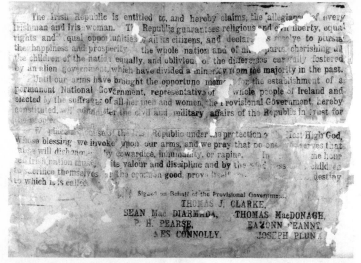

The Irish Republic is entitled to, and hereby claims, the allegiance of every Irishman and Iriswoman. The Republic guarantees religious and civil liberty, equal rights and equal opportunities to all its citizens, and declares its resolve to pursue the happiness and prosperity of the whole nation and of all its parts, cherishing all the children of the nation equally, and oblivious of the differences carefully fostered by an alien government, which have divided a minority from the majority in the past.

Until our arms have brought the opportune moment for the establishment of a permanent National Government, representative of the whole people of Ireland and elected by the suffrages of all her men and women, the Provisional Government, hereby constituted, will administer the civil and military affairs of the Republic in trust for the people.

We place the cause of the Irish Republic under the protection of the Most High God, Whose blessing we invoke upon our arms, and we pray that no one who serves that cause will dishonour it by cowardice, inhumanity, or rapine. In this supreme hour the Irish nation must, by its valour and discipline and by the readiness of its children to sacrifice themselves for the common good, prove itself worthy of the august destiny to which it is called.

Signed on Behalf of the Provisional Government,

THOMAS J. CLARKE,
SEAN Mac DIARMADA,   THOMAS MacDONAGH,
P. H. PEARSE,   EAMONN CEANNT,
JAMES CONNOLLY.   JOSEPH PLUNKETT

Half-print of the Proclamation

Copies of this half-print are very rare but one such copy is in the Kilmainham Gaol Museum.

It has also been suggested that one of the men involved in the printing, Michael J. Molloy, took the final page as a keepsake and that later, when he was a prisoner in Richmond barracks, he chewed it up into small pieces to dispose of it. But this is uncorroborated, and the memorandum prepared for the Government on the subject in October 1953 concludes that this may have been a fabrication (*see pages 43 and 47*).

The monetary value of an original copy of the Proclamation is somewhere in the upper £20,000s. The last recorded price, in December 1998, was £26,000.

4 Historical Perspectives

One of the fascinating historical mysteries of the 1916 Rising had been in relation to the drafting and signing of the Proclamation. Additional information and research has now become available on the subject.

KATHLEEN CLARKE'S MEMOIRS

There is some doubt as to whether the meeting early in Holy Week, when the Military Council met to finalise plans for the Rising and discuss the draft of the Proclamation, was on Tuesday or Wednesday. In her memoir *Revolutionary Woman,* Kathleen Clarke, wife of Tom, says it was on Tuesday. This is her recollection of what her husband told her after the meeting. Though it is not accurate in some details – Pearse, not Clarke, was to be President of the Republic, the Proclamation was not signed, and Eoin MacNeill does not appear in the list of signatories – it is a moving account:

On Tuesday of Holy Week 1916 Tom left the shop in Parnell Square to go to a meeting. I took his place there, and when he was not back by 11 pm I closed the shop and went home, hoping to find him there. He was not, and after a while I began to worry. It was unusually late for him. Our house was at the end of the avenue (Richmond Road), which was not well lighted, and I was always uneasy when he was late, fearing that some night the British might lay in wait for him there and murder him. When he had not arrived by midnight

I put on my hat and coat, and walked the avenue hoping to meet him, but there was no sign of him. I was walking up and down for an hour in a distracted frame of mind; now and then I went into the house to see if my sick son wanted anything, and to see if by any chance he had passed in without my seeing him. The last time I came out I saw him coming up the avenue, and went to meet him. He seemed so joyous and excited, telling me he had great news, that I had not the heart to mention my anxiety and fears to him.

On reaching home we settled down to supper, and during it he told me the great news that the Rising had been arranged for the following Sunday, that a Proclamation had been drawn up to which he was first signatory.

I said, 'That means you will be the first President.'

'Yes,' he said, 'that is what it means.'

Then he told me how the Proclamation was drawn up. Some time before, Pearse had been asked to draft it on the lines intimated to him and submit it to the Military Council. He did, and some changes were made. When it was signed that night it represented the views of all except one, who thought equal opportunities should not be given to women. Except to say that Tom was not that one, my lips are sealed.

Tom then told me that when he was proposed as first signatory he had demurred, saying that he did not think that such an honour should be conferred on him, that he was seeking no honours.

He was very surprised when Thomas MacDonagh rose and said that to his mind no other man was entitled to the honour.

'You, Sir, by your example, your courage, your enthusiasm, have led us younger men to where we are today.'

If Tom Clarke did not agree to accept it, MacDonagh would not sign his name to the Proclamation. 'No man will precede you with my consent.'

Being very much touched by what MacDonagh had said, Tom agreed to sign. He was amazed that anyone should

Thomas J. Clarke and his wife Kathleen

speak so highly of him, being a man of no personal ambitions and no desire for honours. Honours, well, anyone could have them as far as he was concerned. He was the most selfless and unselfish man I ever met; in his house he was the personification of gentleness, joyousness and good temper. I saw him out of temper only a few times in the nearly sixteen years we were together.

At the meeting Tom, as first signatory, was President, Pearse was made Commander-in-Chief of Ireland and Connolly Commander of Dublin. No other positions were created; the other signatories were all members of the Provisional Government. The meeting was held in Mrs Wyse-Power's home at 21 Henry Street. Sean MacDermott was sent from the meeting to see John (Eoin) MacNeill and explain the position to him, and also to ask him to stand in with them and put his name to the Proclamation, and to surrender his position as head of the Irish Volunteers to P.H.

Pearse. He reported back that MacNeill had agreed to go in with them, and that he either signed or agreed to sign the Proclamation, I can't remember which. Immediately after the Rising, I was positive that Tom had said he had signed, but there was so much denial about it that I am now in doubt.

MEMORANDUM OF OCTOBER 1953

A memorandum presented by the Secretary to the Government, N.S. Ó Nuallain, to the then Taoiseach, Eamon de Valera, in October 1953 was released to the National Archives by the Government in 1991. This document (no. A14501), which was prepared following exhaustive enquiries, including consultations with the men who printed the Proclamation, reads as follows:

Apparently, the draft text of the Proclamation in final form was settled at a meeting held in an upstairs room at Liberty Hall early on the morning of Easter Sunday, 1916, at which all seven of those whose names were appended to it were present. The names – but not the signatures – of all seven of the 'signatories' were then appended to it, and the manuscript document was then brought downstairs by James Connolly and Thomas MacDonagh to the printing staff whom Connolly had summoned to be present in the machine-room at Liberty Hall and was handed by Connolly to one of the two compositors (Liam Ó Briain) at about 9 am.

There are only three people now living who we know for certain saw the 'copy' that was supplied to the printing staff: the three members of that staff themselves (the two compositors, Liam Ó Briain and Michael J. Molloy, and the printer, Christopher J. Brady). Of these, only one (Mr. Molloy) has, at any time, alleged that the 'copy' carried the actual signatures of the seven signatories, although, when questioned further on the point, he says that he is 'not so sure' that it bore the actual signatures of the six signatories other than Connolly; the two other members of the printing staff say that the 'copy' did not carry the signatures – but merely the names – of the seven signatories.

All three of the members of the printing staff were familiar with the handwriting of Connolly – Mr Ó Briain says that he was 'particularly familiar' with it – and not one of the three of them (including Mr Molloy) suggests that the body of the 'copy' of the Proclamation was in Connolly's handwriting; the two members of the printing staff, other than Mr Molloy, say that the names of the signatories on the 'copy' were in the same handwriting as that in the body of the Proclamation itself, and it seems in the highest degree unlikely that either of these two members would not have recognised Connolly's signature had he, in fact, signed the 'copy'.

In the nature of things, it seems more likely that the 'copy'

The printers of the Proclamation with Eamon de Valera

supplied to the printing staff would have contained names rather than signatures, having regard to the desirability of having the names reproduced correctly in the printed document. In this connection it is relevant to note (i) that the handwriting of one of the signatories of the Proclamation (Thomas MacDonagh) was almost illegible; and (ii) that, with one exception (Mr O Briain, as regards Pádraig Pearse's handwriting), no member of the printing staff was familiar with the handwriting of any of the signatories other than Connolly. Against this view, however, is the consideration that both Connolly and MacDonagh were there to clear up any doubtful points in the 'copy' when they brought the document to the printing staff and that Connolly, at least, was available for consultation in the matter until about 10 pm, when he read and passed the proofs.

I have never seen it claimed by anybody (apart from the extent to which Mr Molloy makes such a claim) that he saw – or even heard of anybody who saw – an original of the Proclamation bearing the actual signatures of the seven signatories.

It seems rather unlikely that, had there ever been an actual signed original of the Proclamation, it would have been handed out to the printing staff to be used as 'copy'. One would imagine that greater care would have been taken by the signatories themselves to preserve such a document, had it been signed, or that, if it had been used as 'copy', steps would have been taken by the signatories to ensure its return from the printing staff. There must surely have been at least one among the signatories who would have sensed the great historical and sentimental value that would attach to a signed original of the Proclamation – which, of course, is an *a priori* argument in favour of the existence (at some stage) of a signed original – although it should not be forgotten that, at their meeting on Easter Sunday morning at which the final form of the Proclamation was settled by them, the signatories must have had a great many preoccupations (including the situation created by Eoin MacNeill's countermanding order, published in *The Sunday Independent* that morning) transcending in importance that of providing and preserving for posterity an original of a mere document, however valuable that original might have been.

Even the fate of the 'copy' that was used by the printing staff is not altogether clear. Mr Ó Briain says that, as far as he can remember, it was left in the room where he himself and Mr Molloy, the other compositor, set the type; Mr Molloy, however, states that, of the two sheets on which the Proclamation was written (Mr Ó Briain agrees with him on this latter point, although Mr Brady says there was only one sheet), he took away the second sheet (bearing the signatures) from Liberty Hall and subsequently 'destroyed' it in Richmond barracks just before being searched. On being questioned as to how exactly he destroyed it, he says that he chewed and then expectorated it.

Mr Molloy says that he received the following instructions from Connolly regarding the disposal of the 'copy' of the Proclamation: 'Don't leave any copy, especially the single sheet bearing signatures.' This instruction may – notwithstanding all the evidence to the contrary – be indirect evidence in favour of the thesis that the 'copy' bore the actual signatures of the signatories.

In favour of this view it might be argued (i) that, unless the document bore the actual signatures, Connolly had no need to worry about its disposal, as one of the 2,500 printed copies was far more likely to fall into the enemy's hands than the printers' 'copy'; (ii) that a document bearing the actual signatures would probably be far more reliable evidence against the signatories at their courts martial than a mere printed document bearing their names; and (iii) that the instruction related particularly to the portion of the document bearing the signatures (or names) and not to the entire document. Against this view, however, it might be argued (i) that no one who was familiar – as Connolly must have been –

with the condition into which 'copy' gets after being handled by printers (and, particularly, in the circumstances in which the Proclamation was printed) would ordinarily have entrusted to the printers an original signed document to which he attached any value; (ii) that even if, notwithstanding this, the document used by the printers as 'copy' bore the actual signatures of the signatories, Connolly would either have asked for its return with a view to preserving it himself or have given instructions that efforts should be made to reserve it; (iii) that if Connolly had been really anxious about the destruction of the document or of any portion of it, he would have given more explicit instructions on the matter (eg, instructions that the document be burned) than the very general instructions that Mr Molloy says he received from him; (iv) that if Connolly had attached any importance at all to the alleged instructions about the disposal of the 'copy', it is strange that he did not give the instructions to Mr Ó Briain, who claims to have received the 'copy' from Connolly's hands, but not alone did Mr Ó Briain receive no instructions whatever on the matter but he did not hear anyone else receiving such instructions; (v) that Mr Molloy himself admits, on being questioned, that he is not so sure that the 'copy' bore the actual signatures of any of the signatories other than Connolly; (vi) that Mr Molloy's recollection may be at fault and that the instructions may have related to the document as a whole and may not have singled out the portion bearing signatures (or names) for special attention and that the object of the instructions may have been to destroy any evidence against the apparent author of the Proclamation that the manuscript copy in his handwriting would have provided against him; (vii) that Connolly, in some conversation with Mr Molloy – unrelated, perhaps, to the alleged instructions – may have referred loosely to 'signatures', when what he really meant was 'names'; and (viii) that Mr Molloy's story is uncorroborated and that too much reliance should not therefore be placed upon it – in this connection I might add that I have heard that one of the two other members of the printing staff regards Mr Molloy's account of how he destroyed the portion of the 'copy' that he says he took away with him as a fabrication.

My own conclusions from the evidence, on this file, which we have succeeded in collecting are:

(1) that there is no proof that there ever existed a signed original of the Proclamation of Easter Week, 1916, bearing the actual signatures of the seven signatories;

(2) that the only document that might, loosely, be described as the original of the Proclamation was the manuscript 'copy' that was used by the printing staff at Liberty Hall on Easter Sunday, the 23rd April, 1916, and that that document did not contain the actual signatures of the seven signatories of the Proclamation – but merely their names; and

(3) that even this latter document has not survived.

Liam O Briain and Michael J. Molloy, filled in questionnaires about the printing of the Proclamation in March 1953; the originals are in the National Archives. A section from each is reproduced in the following pages.

Section of questionaire filled in by Liam O Briain

1. Did the document bear what appeared to be the actual signature of each of the seven signatories, or did it merely bear each of their names?

   1. It merely bore each of their names.

2. Were all seven of the names in the same handwriting?

   2. Yes.

3. Were these names in the same handwriting as that in the body of the document itself?

   3. Yes.

4. Were the names in ordinary manuscript or in block capitals?

   4. Ordinary manuscript

5. Was the body of the document (apart from the names at the foot) all in one and the same handwriting?

   5. Yes.

6. Were there any corrections in the text?

   6. No.

7. If so, were they in the same or in another hand?

   7. —

8. Were you, at the time, familiar with the handwriting of any of the seven signatories of the Proclamation? And, if so, which of them?

   8. I was particularly familiar with handwriting of James Connolly as I often handled his manuscript. I was also familiar with that of P.H.Pearse.

9. Did you, at the time, know or recognise in whose handwriting the body of the document was written?

   9. At the time I formed the opinion that the handwriting was that of P.H. Pearse.

10. Do you now know in whose handwriting it was?

    10. No. At the same time nothing has since influenced me to change the opinion expressed in para (9) above.

11. Was the handwriting the same as that appearing in the accompanying photostat (of a document written by Pádraic Pearse)?

    11. I could not truthfully state, after the lapse of so many years, that the handwriting is the same as that appearing in photostat accompanying this questionnaire.

It was signed on behalf of the Provisional Govern-
ent by Pearse who signed himself 'Commander-in-
ief of the Forces of the Irish Republic and President
he Provisional Government.'

t is interesting to know how it was possible to have a
es of war bulletins printed and issued from the
neral Post Office during Easter Week. Late on the
ning of Easter Monday, following the occupation,
raig Pearse, James Connolly and Joseph Stanley met
ther and discussed ways and means of issuing
lar daily information to the public to cover the
ities of the Volunteers, to acquaint the citizens with
lopments and, above all, to serve the purpose of
propaganda for the Republican regime.
ere were, of course, many difficulties to be
ome. Pearse strongly advocated the bold course of
g over the premises and plant of the *Irish*
ndent in nearby Abbey Street and producing that
paper in a smaller form as a Provisional
rnment organ. Connolly, however, on military
ds, and Stanley, who saw technical difficulties,
d this suggestion. Connolly's view was that the
andeering and guarding of such a building and
ould make excessive demands on the GPO
.

ight be mentioned here that, according to the
plan for the Rising, Independent House would
en occupied by Republican forces. But the
plans had to be revised due to conflicting orders
nsequent lesser turn-out of volunteers.
ually the whole matter of finding premises and
do such printing was left in the hands of
a Volunteer in the GPO garrison, who under-

Section from that filled in by Michael J. Molloy:

1. Are you quite certain that
   the 'copy' of the Proclamation
   that was given to the compositors
   by James Connolly bore the actual
   signatures of the seven signatories
   (and not merely their names)?

   James Connolly, yes, not so sure of others

2. As you were, at the time, familiar
   with the handwriting of James
   Connolly only, had you any means
   of identifying the signatures of
   the remaining six signatories?

   no.

3. You state : "I took the single
   sheet bearing the signatures with
   me when leaving on instructions".

   (a) Did the instructions to
   which you refer relate
   (i) to your leaving Liberty
   Hall or (ii) to your taking
   with you the sheet mentioned
   by you?

   I would say he meant to destroy

   (b) What exactly were the terms
   of the instructions?

   don't leave any copy, especially the single sheet bearing signatures

   (c) Who gave you the instructions?

   James Connolly

4. You state that you "destroyed" the
   above-mentioned sheet in Richmond
   Barracks just before being searched.
   How exactly did you destroy it?

   when in large hall on gallery I realised then that I had sheet bearing names, I took out copy and was about to tear up, when my fellow prisoner says won't do that, chew it up, and I did so and spat out the bits

5. Have you any idea of what became of
   the other sheet containing the
   remainder of the 'copy' of the
   Proclamation?

   no.

   Signed *Michael J. Molloy*

   Date. *9. March. 1953*

5 The *Irish War News*

On Easter Tuesday a little paper of four in Dublin. *Irish War News* was its ti Pearse's first *communique*, announcing the Provisional Government. A little appeared, which contained the follow

The Provisional Gover
To The
Citizens of Dubli

The Provisional Government of saves the Citizens of Dublin o occasion of the Proclam

SOVEREIGN INDEPENDEN

now in course of being e
Irishmen in a

The valour, self-sacrifice an men and women are about to glorious place among the nati
Ireland's honour has alreac
It remains to vindicate her control.
We have lived to see a claimed. May we live to est our children and our child happiness and prosperity w

49

took to get it done in such a way as would cause little or no drain on the limited military resources. Joseph Stanley was a well-known printer and publisher of many magazines and journals of republican interest. Just then, however, he had neither type nor plant nor premises as he had been raided by British police and military authorities a short time previously at the Gaelic Press, 30 Liffey Street, Dublin, and his plant was broken up and confiscated. Stanley immediately proceeded to look over such plants as would suit his purposes and eventually decided on a man named O'Keeffe at Halston Street, not too far from the GPO. O'Keeffe was soon persuaded that his premises were 'under orders' and Stanley proceeded to assemble a working staff of printers, five in all: the veteran M.S. MacSiubhlaigh (Walker), in charge, who at the age of 69 had walked the whole way from his home in Glasthule to Dublin 'to do his bit somehow'; James O'Sullivan of Denmark Street; Thomas Ryan; Charles Walker, machineman; and Stanley himself as editor and publisher.

The first war bulletin was printed on page four of the *Irish War News* and it really formed the Stop Press column in that rare little journal. The manuscript was written by Pearse. The *War News* was printed on Tuesday morning and sold to the public about noon. (J.J. Bouch, *Irish Press,* 15 April, 1936).

Pearse issued another manifesto on Easter Tuesday. It was a tribute of praise to the men who had fought under him and it was a renunciation of the hope of military success. Pearse addressed the girls and women who had helped in the defence and now ordered them to leave. He told them that without the inspiration of their courage, the Volunteers could not have held out so

52

long. They deserved, he said, a foremost place in the nation's history. He shook hands with each one before they left. (Eithne Coyle, *An Poblacht*, 8 April, 1933.)

Footnote: As events turned out, with the British Army advancing along Abbey Street, James Connolly, with outstanding bravery, led a party of thirty Volunteers from the GPO into Princes Street and through the passage way, Williams Lane, to occupy Independent House as an outpost to counter the British progress. On his way back to the GPO he was badly wounded and collapsed on reaching Princes Street, where he was rescued by his men for medical attention in the GPO.

Princes Street after the Rising

Section from that filled in by Michael J. Molloy:

1. Are you quite certain that
   the 'copy' of the Proclamation
   that was given to the compositors
   by James Connolly bore the actual
   signatures of the seven signatories
   (and not merely their names)?

   James Connolly, yes, not so sure of others

2. As you were, at the time, familiar
   with the handwriting of James
   Connolly only, had you any means
   of identifying the signatures of
   the remaining six signatories?

   no.

3. You state : "I took the single
   sheet bearing the signatures with
   me when leaving on instructions".

   (a) Did the instructions to
       which you refer relate
       (i) to your leaving Liberty
       Hall or (ii) to your taking
       with you the sheet mentioned
       by you?

       I would say to meant to destroy

   (b) What exactly were the terms
       of the instructions?

       don't leave any copy, especially the single sheet bearing signatures

   (c) Who gave you the instructions?

       James Connolly

4. You state that you "destroyed" the
   above-mentioned sheet in Richmond
   Barracks just before being searched.
   How exactly did you destroy it?

   when in large hall on gallery I realised then that I had sheet bearing names, I took out copy and was about to tear up when my decorsprisoner says don't do that, chew it up, and I did so and spat out the bits

5. Have you any idea of what became of
   the other sheet containing the
   remainder of the 'copy' of the
   Proclamation?

   no.

   Signed *Michael. J. Molloy*
   Date.. *9. March. 1953*

IRISH WAR NEWS

THE IRISH REPUBLIC.

VOL. I. No. 1   DUBLIN, TUESDAY, APRIL 25, 1916.   ONE PENNY

"IF THE GERMANS CONQUERED ENGLAND."

In the last number of the "New Statesman" for April 15, an article is published—"If the Germans Conquered England," which has the appearance of a very clever piece of satire written by an Irishman. The writer draws a picture of England under German rule, almost every detail of which exactly fits the case of Ireland at the present day. Some of the sentences are so exquisitely appropriate that it is impossible to believe that the writer had not Ireland in his mind when he wrote them. For instance :—

"England would be constantly irritated by the lofty moral utterances of German statesmen who would assert—quite sincerely, no doubt—that England was free, freer indeed than she had ever been before. Prussian freedom, they would explain, was the only real freedom, and therefore England was free. They would point to the flourishing railways and farms and colleges. They would possibly point to the contingent of M.P.'s, which was permitted, in spite of its deplorable disorderliness, to sit in a permanent minority in the Reichstag. And not only would the Englishman have to listen to a constant flow of speeches of this sort; he would find a respectable official Press secretly bought over by the Government to say the same kind of things over and over, every day of the week. He would find, too, that his children came home from school with new ideas of history. They would ask him if it was true that until the Germans came England had been an unruly country, constantly engaged in civil war. . . . The object of every schoolbook would be to make the English child grow up in the notion that the history of his country was a thing to forget, and that the one bright spot in it was the fact that it had been conquered by cultured Germany."

"If there was a revolt, German statesmen would deliver grave speeches about "disloyalty," "ingratitude." "reckless agitators who would ruin their country's prosperity." . . . Prussian soldiers would be encamped in every barracks—the English army having been sent out of the country to be trained in Germany, or to fight the Chinese—in order to come to the aid of German morality, should English sedition come to blows with it."

"England would be exhorted to abandon her own genius in order to imitate the genius of her conquerors, to forget her own history for a larger history, to give up her own language for a "universal" language—in other words, to destroy her household gods one by one, and put in their place"

5 The *Irish War News*

On Easter Tuesday a little paper of four pages appeared in Dublin. *Irish War News* was its title. It contained Pearse's first *communique,* announcing the setting up of the Provisional Government. A little later a single sheet appeared, which contained the following manifesto:

The Provisional Government
To The
Citizens of Dublin

The Provisional Government of the Irish Republic salutes the Citizens of Dublin on the momentous occasion of the Proclamation of a

SOVEREIGN INDEPENDENT IRISH STATE

now in course of being established by
Irishmen in arms

The valour, self-sacrifice and discipline of Irish men and women are about to win for our country a glorious place among the nations.

Ireland's honour has already been redeemed;

It remains to vindicate her wisdom and her self-control.

We have lived to see an Irish Republic proclaimed. May we live to establish it firmly, and may our children and our children's children enjoy the happiness and prosperity which freedom will bring.

It was signed on behalf of the Provisional Government by Pearse who signed himself 'Commander-in-Chief of the Forces of the Irish Republic and President of the Provisional Government.'

It is interesting to know how it was possible to have a series of war bulletins printed and issued from the General Post Office during Easter Week. Late on the evening of Easter Monday, following the occupation, Pádraig Pearse, James Connolly and Joseph Stanley met together and discussed ways and means of issuing regular daily information to the public to cover the activities of the Volunteers, to acquaint the citizens with developments and, above all, to serve the purpose of active propaganda for the Republican regime.

There were, of course, many difficulties to be overcome. Pearse strongly advocated the bold course of taking over the premises and plant of the *Irish Independent* in nearby Abbey Street and producing that newspaper in a smaller form as a Provisional Government organ. Connolly, however, on military grounds, and Stanley, who saw technical difficulties, opposed this suggestion. Connolly's view was that the commandeering and guarding of such a building and staff would make excessive demands on the GPO garrison.

It might be mentioned here that, according to the original plan for the Rising, Independent House would have been occupied by Republican forces. But the original plans had to be revised due to conflicting orders and a consequent lesser turn-out of volunteers.

Eventually the whole matter of finding premises and plant to do such printing was left in the hands of Stanley, a Volunteer in the GPO garrison, who undertook to get it done in such a way as would cause little or no drain on the limited military resources. Joseph Stanley was a well-known printer and publisher of many magazines and journals of republican interest. Just then, however, he had neither type nor plant nor premises as he had been raided by British police and military authorities a short time previously at the Gaelic Press, 30 Liffey Street, Dublin, and his plant was broken up and confiscated. Stanley immediately proceeded to look over such plants as would suit his purposes and eventually decided on a man named O'Keeffe at Halston Street, not too far from the GPO. O'Keeffe was soon persuaded that his premises were 'under orders' and Stanley proceeded to assemble a working staff of printers, five in all: the veteran M.S. MacSiubhlaigh (Walker), in charge, who at the age of 69 had walked the whole way from his home in Glasthule to Dublin 'to do his bit somehow'; James O'Sullivan of Denmark Street; Thomas Ryan; Charles Walker, machineman; and Stanley himself as editor and publisher.

The first war bulletin was printed on page four of the *Irish War News* and it really formed the Stop Press column in that rare little journal. The manuscript was written by Pearse. The *War News* was printed on Tuesday morning and sold to the public about noon. (J.J. Bouch, *Irish Press,* 15 April, 1936).

Pearse issued another manifesto on Easter Tuesday. It was a tribute of praise to the men who had fought under him and it was a renunciation of the hope of military success. Pearse addressed the girls and women who had helped in the defence and now ordered them to leave. He told them that without the inspiration of their courage, the Volunteers could not have held out so long. They deserved, he said, a foremost place in the nation's history. He shook hands with each one before they left. (Eithne Coyle, *An Poblacht,* 8 April, 1933.)

Footnote: As events turned out, with the British Army advancing along Abbey Street, James Connolly, with outstanding bravery, led a party of thirty Volunteers from the GPO into Princes Street and through the passage way, Williams Lane, to occupy Independent House as an outpost to counter the British progress. On his way back to the GPO he was badly wounded and collapsed on reaching Princes Street, where he was rescued by his men for medical attention in the GPO.

Princes Street after the Rising

The surrender of Pearse.

6 Aftermath

'We hereby proclaim the Irish Republic as a Sovereign Independent State, and we pledge our lives and the lives of our comrades-in-arms to the cause of its freedom, of its welfare, and of its exaltation among the nations.'

THE PROCLAMATION OF 1916

The official figures regarding the number of men and women arrested after the Rising are those issued by the British Military headquarters in Dublin on 11 July 1916. The total was 3,226; 3,149 men and 77 women.

The suspected leaders were court-martialled; 160 were convicted and sentenced and 23 acquitted. Over half of the rest – 1,862 – were interned in various detention barracks in England, Scotland and Wales; the remaining 1,104 were released. Of the women, 72 were released and five interned.

British military casualties were 130 killed in action and 365 wounded.

Of the civilians killed, no accurate computation was made but hospital lists provided information. According to a report in the *Irish Independent* on 8 May 1916, 250 persons whose deaths occurred as a result of bullet or gunshot wounds, or were otherwise attributable to the Rising, were buried in Glasnevin cemetery, 49 in Deans Grange, and 24 in Mount Jerome. There were 32 unidentified civilian casualties.

The official Roll of Honour is on pages 58 to 86.

Dublin city centre after the Rising.

William Pearse

Michael O'Hanrahan

Michael Mallin

Sean Heuston

John MacBride

Con Colbert

Executed in Kilmainham Gaol

P.H. Pearse
Thomas J. Clarke
Thomas MacDonagh
Joseph Plunkett
Edward Daly
William Pearse
Michael O'Hanrahan

John MacBride
Eamonn Ceannt
Michael Mallin
Con Colbert
Sean Heuston
Sean MacDiarmada
James Connolly

Volunteers Killed in Action

John Adams
Thomas Allen
William Burke
Andrew Byrne
James Byrne
Louis Byrne
Charles Carrigan
Philip Clarke
Sean Connolly
James Corcoran
Edward Cosgrave
Edward Costello
John Costello
Henry Coyle
John Crenigan
John Cromien
Charles Darcy
Brendan Donelan
Patrick Doyle
John Dwan
Edward Ennis
Patrick Farrell
James Fox
George Geoghegan
John Healy

Sean Howard
Sean Hurley
John Keely
Gerard Keogh
Richard Kent
Francis Macken
Peadar Macken
Michael Malone
Peter Manning
James McCormack
William McDowell
Michael Mulvihill
Richard Murphy
Daniel Murray
Richard O'Carroll
Patrick O'Connor
Patrick O'Flanagan
John O'Grady
The O'Rahilly
John O'Reilly
Thomas O'Reilly
John Owens
James Quinn
Thomas Rafferty
George Reynolds

Frederick Ryan
Patrick Shortis
John Traynor
Edward Walsh

Philip Walshe
Thomas Weafer
Patrick Whelan
Peter Wilson

Volunteers Drowned on Active Service

Con Keating   Charles Monaghan   Donal Sheehan

Executed in Cork Jail

Thomas Kent

Executed in Pentonville Prison, London

Roger Casement

Sentenced to Death but Commuted to Penal Servitude

Thomas Ashe
Charles Bevan
Thomas Bevan
Michael Brady
James Brennan
Maurice Brennan
Robert Brennan
Fred Brooks
James Burke
J. Byrne
Peader Clancy
J. Clarke
P. Coleman
William P. Corrigan
Philip B. Cosgrave
William Cosgrave
John F. Cullen
James Dempsey
Michael de Lacy

Eamon de Valera
John Doherty
J. Dorrington
John Downey
Gerald Doyle
James Doyle
John R. Etchingham
John Faulkner
Peter Galligan
Thomas Hunter
George Irvine
P. Kelly
R. Kelly
Richard F. King
Frank Lawless
James Lawless
George Levins
Diarmuid Lynch
Fionan Lynch

John McArdle
John McGarry
Patrick McNestry
Constance G. Markievics
William Meehan
James Melinm
Michael Mervyn
Bryan Molloy
G. Monks
James Morrissey
J. Norton
John O'Brien
Denis O'Callaghan
William O'Dea
C. O'Donovan

Henry O'Hanlon
T. O'Kelly
James O'Sullivan
T. Peppard
George Plunkett
John Plunkett
James Rafter
John J. Reid
John Shouldice
P. Emmet Sweeney
William Tobin
James Joseph Walsh
Thomas Walsh
John Williams
P. Wilson

W. Wilson

Edward Daly

Eamon de Valera

7 Roll of Honour

The 1916 Roll of Honour assembled by the National Museum some years after the Rising is regarded as the definitive record. The names are arranged by garrison.

GPO, O'Connell Street

Adrien, Mary
Agnew, Arthur P.

Barry, Mrs Tom
Behan, Michael
Bermingham, Andrew J.
Bermingham, John
Billings, Joseph
Bird, Patrick
Boland, Edmund
Boland, Harry
Boland, Michael
Bracken, Peadar
Brady, Michael
Breen, Liam
Brophy, Daniel
Bulfinn, Eamonn
Burke, Frank
Burke, Nicholas
Byrne, Catherine
Byrne, Christopher
Byrne, Edward
Byrne, James
Byrne, John C.

Byrne, Louis
Byrne, Patrick J.
Byrne, Peter S.
Byrne, Thomas F.

Caddell, Patrick
Caldwell, Patrick
Callan, Joseph
Canny, Daniel
Carmichael, Bernard
Carpenter, Peter
Carpenter, Walter P.
Cassells, James
Cassidy, Joseph P.
Chadwick, Mrs May
Clarke, Thomas J.
Clinch, P.J.
Coate, John
Cole, Sean
Colgain, Padraic
Colley, Harry
Collins, Michael
Connaughton, Patrick
Connolly, Brigid

Connolly, James
Conroy, Andrew
Conway, Sean S.
Conway, Winifred
Corbally, Laurence
Corbally, Richard
Corbally, Thomas
Corrigan, Charles
Corrigan, James
Courtney, Daniel
Cowley, Michael
Coyle, Harry
Craven, Thomas
Cripps, Joseph A.
Croft, Gerard
Croke, Michael
Croke, Thomas
Cullen, William F.
Cummins, Tom

Dalton, Patrick
Daly, Denis
Daly, Liam
Daly, Seamus
de Burca, Aoife
de Stainear, Michael
Dennahy, Patrick
Derham, Joseph
Devereux, Patrick
Devine, Francis
Devine, Thomas W.
Devoy, Seamus
Donnelly, Charles
Donnelly, Patrick
Dore, Eamon T.
Dore, Mrs Nora Daly

Dowling, Michael
Doyle, J.J.
Doyle, John J.
Doyle, John
Doyle, John
Doyle, Peter
Duffy, Edward
Duffy, Joseph
Dunne, Francis
Dunne, John
Dunne, Joseph
Dunne, Thomas
Dwyer, Michael
Dyas, Albert

Early, John
English, Maire
English, Patrick
Ennis, Thomas

Finegan, Michael
Fitzgerald, Desmond
Fitzharris, John J.
Fitzpatrick, Andrew J.
Flanagan, Matthew
Flanagan, Rev John CC
Flynn, Ignatius
Fogarty, Thomas
Fox, Michael
Frick, Bernard
Furlong, Andrew

Gahan, Joseph
Gallagher, Patrick
Galligan, Paul
Gannon, Henry
Garland, Patrick

Gavan, John J.
Gethings, Lucie
Gibson, Richard
Giffney, Michael
Gleeson, Joseph
Gleeson, Martin
Gogan, Richard P.
Good, Alfred

Harris, Thomas
Hayes, J.J.
Healy, Richard
Heffernan, Michael
Hegarty, Sean
Henderson, Frank
Higgins, Frederick P.
Higgins, Peter
Hoey, Patricia
Hughes, Patrick
Hughes, T.
Hutchinson, Joseph

Hynes, John F.

Inglis, Frainnc

Jackson, P.
Jenkinson, Margaret (née Walsh)
Jones, Thomas
Joyce, Brian

Kavanagh, Seamus
Kealy, John
Kearney, Thomas
Kearns, Hubert
Keating, Con
Keeling, Christopher
Kelly Barber, Kathleen J.
Kelly, Edward
Kelly, Frank
Kelly, John
Kelly, Joseph
Kennan, Austin

The GPO after the Rising

Kennedy, Luke
Kenny, Henry V.
Kenny, James
Kenny, John
Kenny, Michael
Keogh, Bernard
Keogh, Michael
Kerr, Sean
Kerwan, P.
Killeen, Robert
Kilmartin, P.
King, George
King, John
King, Patrick
King, Samuel
Knightly, Michael

Lambert, Bridget
Lawless, Edward
Lawless, Mary
Leahy, Thomas
Ledwith, Joseph
Lee, Hugh
Lee, Joseph
Lemass, Noel
Lemass, Sean F.
Lynch, Diarmuid
Lynch, John
Lynch, Martin
Lynch, Patrick Leo

McAuliffe, Gearoid
McCabe, Kevin J.
McCleane, William J.
MacCraic, Micheal
McCrea, Patrick
MacDermott, Rory

MacDiarmada, Sean
McDonagh, Joseph
MacDonnell, John
MacDowell, Maeve C.
McElligott, J.J.
McEntagart, John
McEntee, Sean
McEvoy, Dominick
McEvoy, Thomas
McGallogly, James
McGallogly, John
McGarry, Sean
McGinley, C.
McGinley, Liam
McGinley, Patrick
McGinn, Conway
McGinty, Mrs L. (née
    Burke)
McGrane, Christopher
McGrath, Patrick J. (jun)
McGrath, Patrick J. (sen)
McGrath, Thomas
Macken, Frank
MacKey, Leo
MacKey, Michael
MacLaughlin, Dr D.
McLoughlin, Mary
MacMahon, Patrick
McMahon, Donal
McMahon, Sean
McManus, Patrick
MacMullen, Brian
McNally, John
MacNeive, Liam
McPartland, Frank
McPartlin, Peter C.

MacSharry, M. (née Fagan)
Madden, Sean
Maguire, J.
Maguire, Matthew
Mahon, Patrick
Mahon, P.J.
Mahon, Thomas
Malone, J.J.
Mangan, Thomas
Manning, Henry
Mapotar, Maire
Mairé, Louis
Mason, Thomas
Matthew, Caffrey
Meagher, Patrick
Mhic Ruidigh, Sorcha
Milroy, Sean
Mooney, Patrick
Moore, Edward J.
Mulcahy, Mary J.
Mulvey, W.P.
Mulvihill, Michael
Murphy, Charles
Murphy, Fintan
Murphy, Mrs Gertie
Murphy, Kathleen
Murphy, Martha
Murphy, Michael
Murphy, R.J.
Murphy, Stephen
Murray, Eileen
Murray, P.J.
Murray, Thomas
Murtagh, Francis

Ni Ainle, Maire

Ni Dhubhthaigh, Luise G.
Ni Foghludha, Nora
Ni Riain, Aine
Noone, Mrs Ellen
Norton, James
Nugent, Michael
Nugent, Patrick

O Bhaonain, Seamus
O Briain, Eoghan
O Briain, Tomas
O'Brien, John
O'Brien, Matt
O'Brien, Michael
O Buachalla, Domhnall
O'Byrne, James
O'Byrne, James
O Caoimh, Padraig
O'Carroll, Kevin
O Ceallaigh, Eamonn
O Cearbhail, Peadar
O'Connell, Mary
O'Connor, James
O'Connor, Johnny
O'Connor, Patrick
O'Connor, Peter
O Donnchadha, Tomas
O'Gorman, Liam
O'Hanrahan, Mary
O'Higgins, Annie
O'Kelly, Fergus F.
O'Kelly, Joseph
O'Kelly, Sean T.
O'Mahony, Eamon J.
O'Mahony, Matthew
Oman, George

Interior of the GPO

O'Moore, Donough
O Mordha, Padraig
O Murchadha, Peadar
O Murchu, Miceal
O'Neill, James
O'Neill, John
O'Neill, John
O'Neill, Maire
O'Neill, Seamus
O Nunain, Sean
O'Rahilly, The
O Raogain, Liam
O'Reilly, Cathleen
O'Reilly, J.K.
O'Reilly, John
O'Reilly, Joseph
O'Reilly, Mary (Mrs Corcoran)

O'Reilly, M.W.
O'Reilly, Thomas
O Riain, Liam
O Riain, Seamus (Dr Jim Ryan)
O'Sullivan, Gearoid
O'Sullivan, James
O'Sullivan, Laura Daly
O'Toole, William

Parnell, Matthew
Pearse, P.H.
Pearse, William
Pedlar, Liam
Plunkett, Joseph
Price, Sean
Purcell, C.

Quinn, Margaret

Rafferty, Mrs M.J. (née Walsh)
Rankin, Patrick
Redmond, Andy
Redmond, Annie
Reid, John
Reilly, Matthew
Reynolds, John R.
Reynolds, Molly
Reynolds, Peter J.
Richards, Bridie
Ridgeway, Harry
Ring, Christopher
Ring, Joseph
Ring, Patrick
Robinson, Seamus
Roche, Thomas J.
Roche, William
Rossiter, C.
Roth, Thomas
Ryan, Oliver
Ryan, Phyllis
Ryan, Thomas

Saurin, Charles
Scollan, J.J.
Scullin, Francis
Scullin, Patrick
Seville, James
Sexton, James
Sheridan, Frank
Sheridan, James
Shields, Arthur
Shortis, Patrick
Simpson, Tilley
Slater, Birdie (née Walsh)

Slattery, Peader
Slevin, Mrs M.J. (née Stapleton)
Smith, Charles
Smyth, Lucy (Mrs Tom Byrne)
Stafford Brooks, Christine
Stanley, Joseph
Steinmayer, Charles
Stephenson, Patrick J.
Stritch, Jim
Stynes, Mrs Ellen (née Lambert)
Supple, Padraig
Swan, Anthony
Sweeney, James
Sweeney, Joseph
Sweeney, Patrick

Tallon, Christopher
Tallon, James
Tannam, Liam
Thornton, Frank
Thornton, Hugh
Thornton, Patrick
Tobin, Annie (Mrs Soalfield)
Toomey, Joseph
Toomey, Stasia (Mrs S. Byrne)
Traynor, Oscar
Treston, Cathleen
Trimble, Joseph
Tuohy, Dr J.J.
Tuohy, Patrick
Turner, Cormac

Turner, Francis
Turner, Joseph
Twamley, John J.
Tyrrell, Timothy

Ui Faoithe, Brigid Bean
Ui Glasam, Veronica (née
  Ni Riain)

Wade, Michael
Walker, Charles
Walpole, R.H.
Walsh, Christopher
Walsh, Edward

Walsh, James Joseph
Walsh, Mark
Wardock, James
Weafer, Patrick
Weafer, Thomas
Wheatley, Thomas
Whelan, Joseph
White, John J.
White, Michael
Willis, Henry
Wisely, Esther (Mrs S.
  O'Moore)
Wren, James

Boland's Mills

Banks, Henry
Banks, Sean
Bermingham, John
Boylan, Stephen
Bracken, John
Bracken, John (jun)
Breen, Sean
Brennan, Patrick
Brennan, Patrick
Breslin, Toby
Brown, William
Browne, James
Browne, William
Burton, Frederick
Byrne, C.
Byrne, Dermot
Byrne, Henry
Byrne, John
Byrne, Joseph
Byrne, Michael

Byrne, Michael
Byrne, Michael
Byrne, Patrick
Byrne, Patrick
Byrne, Peter
Byrne, Thomas

Carroll, Dudley
Casey, Leo
Cassidy, Thomas
Coates, Peter
Colgan, Daniel
Conroy, William
Cooper, Robert
Cosgrave, John
Coyne, Thomas
Cullen, Michael
Cullen, Sean

Daly, James
de Valera, Eamon

Boland's Mills

Donnelly, Simon
Donovan, Michael
Doyle, James
Doyle, James H.
Doyle, Patrick
Doyle, Patrick
Doyle, Seamus
Dunne, John

Ennis, Edward

Finn, Timothy
FitzGerald, James
Fitzgerald, Leo
Fitzgerald, Thomas
Fitzgerald, Wm
Flanagan, Patrick
Fleming, Michael
Flynn, John A.
Fullam, Thomas

Gill, James T.
Gordon, Edward
Grace, James Joseph
Griffin, Martin
Guilfoyle, Joseph

Henry, James
Hickey, Michael
Humphreys, Richard

Jackson, Francis
Jackson, Joseph

Kavanagh, James
Kavanagh, Liam
Kavanagh, Peadar
Kelly, Patrick
Kelly, Thomas
Kenny, Charles
Kinsella, John

Kirwan, Edward

Lalor, Eamon
Leonard, Edward
Liffiroi, Leo
Lyons, Geo A.

Mac an Bhaird, Padraig
McArdle, Owen
McBride, Patrick
McCabe, Liam
McCaibe, Liam
McCabe, Patrick
McCarthy, Bernard
McCarthy, Michael
McCurran, Joseph
McDermott, Joseph
McDermott, Sean
McDonnell, Andrew
MacDowell, Cathal
McDowell, Patrick
McEffoy, Sean
MacGhaill, Padraig
Mac Giolla Bhridge, Padraig

Mac Giollaphol, Sean
Macken, Peader
MacMahon, Sean
Mac Uinseann, Sean
Mallon, James
Malone, Michael
Malone, Robert
Martin, Joe
Meagher, Michael
Meagher, Patrick
Merriman, Michael
Molloy, Joseph
Mullen, Murtagh Patrick
Murphy, Christopher J.
Murphy, John J.
Murphy, Liam
Murphy, Richard
Murray, Frank
Murray, Michael
Murray, Seamus

Nolan, P.
Nolan, Patrick

Surrender of Eamon de Valera

Nugent, John
Nugent, Joseph

O'Brien, William
O Broin, Liam
O'Byrne, Joseph
O'Byrne, Tom
O Caomhanaigh, Michael
O'Connor, Joe
O'Connor, Joseph
O Cuirbre, Cristoir
O'Donoghue, Denis
O Duinn, Sean
O'Grady, Anthony
O'Hanlon, John
O hAodha, A.
O'Keeffe, Sean
O Leannain, Michael
O Meadra, Peadar
O'Neill, Andrew
O'Reilly, Christopher
O'Reilly, Patrick
O'Rourke, Thomas
O Scolaige, Tomas
O'Shea, Sean
O'Treacy, Seamus

Pearle, Richard
Peate, Thomas
Peelo, Denis

Pender, James
Porter, Owen
Power, Patrick
Purfield, James

Quin, Thomas
Quinn, Sean
Raftis, Liam
Redican, James
Reid, John J.
Reid, Patrick
Reynolds, George
Roe, Patrick
Roe, William C.
Rownan, William
Ryan, Cornelius

Stanley, Liam
Stokes, John J.

Tannam, Miceal
Thompson, Alexander
Traynor, Thomas

Walker, John
Walsh, James
Walsh, Thomas
Waters, James
Whelan, Patrick
Williams, Patrick
Woodcock, William

Cabra Bridge

Blanchfield, Thomas Patrick
Brennan, Maurice
Dempsey, James
Dunne, Patrick

Faulkiner, John
McArdle, John
O Higgins, James
O'Reilly, Samuel P.

City Hall

Barrett, Mrs Kathleen
Brady, Brigid
Brady, Christopher
Byrne, John
Byrne, John
Byrne, Louis
Byrne, Patrick

Connolly, Mattie
Connolly, Sean
Coyle, Thomas

Daly, Thomas
D'Arcy, Charles

Elmes, E.
Farrell, Denis
Finlay, John
Flynn, Kathleen

Geoghegan, George

Halpin, William
Halpin, William
Hanratty, Mrs Emily

Kain, Thomas
Kelly, Bessie
King, Arthur

King, George
King, S.

Lambert, James
McDonnell, James
Molony, Helena
Mullally, Michael

Nelson, Thomas
Nolan, John
Norgrove, Annie

O'Duffy, Brigid (née Davis)
O'Dwyer, James
O'Keeffe, John C.
O'Leary, Philip
Oman, William
O'Reilly, John
O'Reilly, John

Poole, John

Seery, James
Sexton, Michael
Shanahan, Jennie

Walsh, Thomas
Williams, Patrick Joseph
Winstanley, Henry

Four Courts

Allen, Mary (née Murray)
Allen, Thomas
Archer, Liam

Beaslai, Piaras
Beggs, Robert

Begley, Daniel J.
Bent, John
Bevan, Charles S.
Bevan, James
Bevan, Joseph
Bevan, Thomas J.

Bibby, Fr Albert OMC
Bird, James
Blackhead, Kathleen (née Kenny)
Blanchfield, Peter
Brabazon, Joseph
Breslin, James
Breslin, Peadar
Breslin, Thomas
Bridgeman, Edward
Burns, James
Butler, George
Byrne, Teresa (née Healy)
Byrne, Ambrose
Byrne, Charles
Byrne, John
Byrne, Laurence
Byrne, Mary
Byrne, Patrick
Byrne, Sean
Byrne, Seamus
Byrne, William

Cahill, James
Callender, Ignatius
Campbell, M.J.
Carron, Maire
Cassidy, Thomas
Catlin, John Patrick
Clancy, Peadar
Clarke, James
Cody, Sean
Coffey, Joseph
Coghlan, Francis X.
Coleton, Elizabeth (née Murnane)

Collins, Maurice
Condron, Luke
Conroy, James (sen)
Copeland, Mgt (née Byrne)
Cosgrove, Michael
Costigan, Nellie (née Ennis)
Cox, Redmond
Coyle, William
Cullen, Joseph
Cullen, Thomas

Daly, Edward
Darker, Michael
Delemere, Edward
Dempsey, James
Derham, Michael
Derrington, Liam
Doggett, Christopher
Domican, John
Donohoe, Sylvester
Dowling, Andrew
Dowling, John
Dowling, Thomas
Doyle, John
Doyle, Thomas J.
Duffy, Christopher
Duggan, E.J.
Duggan, May (née Kavanagh)
Dunn (or Dunne), Thomas
Dwan, John

Edwards, Michael
Ellis, Sean

Fagan, John
Fagan, Michael

The Four Courts

Fahy, Anna
Fahy, Frank
Farrell, John
Farrell, Patrick
Farrell, Thomas
Farrelly, Christopher
Farrelly, Sean
Farren, Stephen
Feeney, Gerald
Fitzpatrick, Denis
Flood, Sean
Fogarty, John
Fogarty, Patrick

Forde, Sean
Foy, Frederick
Frawley, Denis

Gahan, Mathew
Gaynor, Arthur
Geraghty, Sean
Gilsenan, Patrick
Graham, James
Green, Patrick
Griffith, William
Grimley, Michael

Halpin, John

Halpin, Peadar
Harding, Frank
Harnett, Alf
Hamill, Thomas
Healy, Cathleen
Healy, Peadar
Henderson, Thomas
Hendrick, Edward
Hendrick, James Joseph
Heron, Aine
Hogan, P.J.
Hogan, William Conor
Howard, Con
Howard, Sean
Howlett, Michael
Hurley, Sean
Hyland, Thomas
Hynes, Sean

Kavanagh, James
Kavanagh, James
Kearns, Patrick
Keating, Pauline (née Morkan)
Kelly, Joseph
Kelly, Michael
Kelly, Patrick
Kennedy, Sean
Kennedy, James J.
Kennedy, John
Kenny, John
Kenny, John

Laffan, Nicholas
Lawlor, Mary (née O'Carroll)
Lawlor, Frank
Lawlor, Larry

Lawlor, Sean
Ledwith, Emily (nee Elliott)
Ledwith, Peter
Leggett, Robert
Lennon, Nicholas
Lowe, Arnold
Lynch, Gilbert
Lyons, Charles
Lyons, Edward
Lyons, John E

Mac an Bhaird, Gilbert
McCabe, Frank
McCann, Thomas J.
McCormack, Christopher J.
McCormack, John
McDonnell, Thomas
MacDonough, Joseph
McEvatt, Louis
McGill, Joseph
McGuinness, Catherine
McGuinness, Joseph
McGuinness, Rose
Macken, Patrick
McKeon, Brigid (née Murrane)
McKeon, Owen
McKeon, William
McLoughlin, Peter
Mac Meachtaigh, M.
MacMearmar, Maighnas
McMenarigh, Joseph
McNally, Francis
MacNamara, Patrick
McNamara, James
McNestry, Patrick

McNulty, Micheal
McNulty, Peadar
McQuaile, May (née Moloney)
Magee, Michael
Maguire, Thomas
Manning, Peadar
Martin, Kathleen
Mason, Frank
Mason, G.
Meade, Henry
Meade, Walter
Meade, William
Merrigan, Michael
Merrigan, Thomas
Mooney, Patrick
Morkan, Eamon
Morkan, Phyllis
Mulkearns, James J.
Mullen, Peter
Munroe, Thomas J.
Murnane, Liam
Murnane, Margaret (née Martin)
Murphy, Eileen (née Walsh)
Murphy, Francis Charles
Murphy, Hubert J.
Murphy, Martin
Murphy, Michael
Murphy, William
Murray, Joseph M.
Murtagh, Laurence J.
Murtagh, Patrick
Musgrave, Denis J.

Neary, Denis

Neilan, Arthur
Nevin, Patrick
Ni Briain, Eilis (née Elliot)

O Braonain, Eamonn
O Briain, Sean
O Briain, Thomas
O'Brien, Michael
O'Brien, Patrick
O'Brien, Patrick
O Canain, Tomas
O'Carroll, Annie (née O'Keeffe)
O'Carroll, Mary (née O'Sullivan)
O'Carroll, Michael
O'Carroll, Robert
O'Carroll, Sean
O Ceallachain, Donnchadh
O Cearbhaill, Liam
O Cearbhaill, Peadar
O'Conaill, Mort
O Conallan, M.
O'Connor, John
O'Connor, John S.
O'Connor, Patrick J.
O'Dea, Michael
O'Doherty, Fionan
O'Doherty, Liam
O Donnabhain, Conn
O'Duffy, Sean M.
O'Flanagan, Francis
O'Flanagan, George
O'Flanagan, Maurice
O'Flanagan, Michael
O'Flanagan, Patrick

O Foghludha, Micheal
O'Gorman, Liam
O'Gorman, Mary Christina
  (née Hayes)
O'Hanlon, Bernard
O'Hanlon, Patrick
O hEigeartaigh, Diarmuid
O'Kelly, Michael
O'Leary, Patrick Joseph
O Loingsigh, Miceal
O Loinsigh, Fionan
Oman, Robert
O'Moore, Sean
O Murchadha, Brian
O Murchadha, Cristoir
O Murchadha, Michael
O'Neill, Joseph
O'Neill, Michael
O'Neill, Patrick Francis
O'Neill, William
O Nuallain, Tomas
O'Reardan, Michael
O'Reilly, Luke J.
O'Reilly, Peter
O'Reilly, Thomas
O Riain, Liam S.
O Scollaighe, Michael
O Sullivan, James

Parker, Ellen (née
  O'Flanagan)
Pollard, Frank D.
Pollard, Louisa (née
  O'Sullivan)
Pollard, Stephen
Prendergast, Sean

Rawley, Albert Sylvester
Regan, Laurence
Reid, Sean
Richmond, John
Roache, Joseph
Roche, Michael Joseph
Ryan, William

Sanders, Michael
Savage, Martin
Scully, William
Sheely, Charles
Sheerin, Thomas P.
Sheridan, James
Sheridan, John
Shouldice, Frank
Shouldice, Jack
Siupteal, Liam
Smart, Thomas
Stephenson, Mary
Swan, Patrick
Sweeney, Joseph

Thornton, Brigid (née
  Lyons)
Tierney, Michael
Tobin, Liam
Tobin, Michael
Travers, Edward

Ui Chonnallan, Peig Bean
Ui Conaill, Eilis (née Ni
  Riain)

Walsh, James
Walsh, Philip
Ward, George

Ward, Sean
Whelan, George

Williams, John J.
Wilson, Mark

Jacob's Factory

Barrett, James
Barrett, William
Begley, Joseph
Bermingham, John
Berry, William
Blake, William J.
Brady, Francis
Brady, Patrick
Brennan, Laurence
Breslin, Patrick
Brian, John
Buckley, William J.
Burke, Thomas
Byrne, Joseph
Byrne, Vincent
Byrne, William

Carberry, James
Carney, Francis Joseph
Cassells, James
Chambers, Daniel
Christie, Peter
Colbert, Sean
Comerford, Andrew
Cotter, Joseph
Cotter, Richard
Cotter, Thomas
Cullen, Peter
Cunningham, James

Darcy, Patrick Leo
de Bruin, Seosamh

Deegan, Maire
Deegan, Sean
Dolan, Peter
Doyle, Patrick
Doyle, Thomas
Drumm, Thomas

Ellis, Samuel
Ennis, Christopher
Ennis, Michael

Farrell, James
Farrelly, Christopher
Fitzpatrick, Michael
Furlong, John
Furlong, Mathew

Gahan, Tadhg
Gleeson, Dr P. (or D.P.)
Goulding, Charles
Goulding, James
Grattan, Richard
Gregory, John

Hunter, Thomas

Joyce, John
Joyce, Joseph James

Kavanagh, Daniel
Kealy, Sara
Kearns, Frank
Kearns, John
Kearns, Joseph

Jacob's Factory

Kearns, Tom
Kelly, Henry

Kelly, John E.
Kenny, James

Keogh, Thomas
King, Sean

Lake, John Watson
Lane, Edward
Lane, Kathleen (née
  McCarthy)
Lanigan, Patrick
Lawless, M.
Long, Patrick
Losty, Thomas
Love, Michael
Lynch, Sean
Lynch, William
Lyons, Edward

MacAodha, Saoirse
MacBride, John
MacDaibhis, Risteard
McDermott, Owen
MacDonagh, John
MacDonagh, Thomas
McDonnell, Matthew
McDonnell, Patrick
McEvoy, Patrick
McGlure, John
McGrane, Thomas
McGrath, Daniel
McKee, Richard
MacMahon, Bernard J.
McParland, James
Magee, Teresa
Maher, William
Manning, Patrick
Meade, Michael
Meade, Owen
Meldon, John

Meldon, Thomas
Molloy, Richard
Moran, Patrick
Mullen, Martin
Murphy, John J.

Nic Siubhlaigh, Maire
Nolan, Patrick

O Beolain, Gearoid
O'Byrne, Patrick
O Cahill, Art
O'Carroll, James Joseph
O'Carroll, James
O'Carroll, Richard
O Casaigh, Seamus
O Cathalain, Padraig
O Ceallachain, Sean
O Ceallaigh, Padraig
O Ceallaigh, Seosamh S
O Cearnaigh, Peader
O'Connell, Patrick
O Cortain, Michael
O'Donnell, Christopher
O'Donnell, James
O'Grady, John
O'Hagan, Annie
O'Hagan, Hugh
O'Hanrahan, Edward
O'Hanrahan, Henry
O'Hanrahan, Joseph
O'Hanrahan, Michael
O'Hanrahan O'Reilly, Lily
O hAodh, Michael
O hAódha, Seamus
O'Malley, Christopher
O Maoilfinn, Seamus

80

O Murain, Seamus
O'Neill, Cecilia (née Conroy)
O'Reilly, Patrick
O'Reilly, Thomas
O Riordain, Domhnall
O'Rorke, Frederick
O'Rourke, John
O'Rourke, Michael
O Ruairc, Sean T.
O Ruairc, Tomas
O'Shea, Dermot
O'Shea, James
O'Torma, Seosamh

Phelan, Michael J.
Pollard, Josephine (née Daly)
Pollard, Kathleen (née McDonald)
Pounch, James S.
Price, Eamon
Pugh, Thomas

Redmond, Patrick
Redmond, William J.
Reynolds, John A.
Roche, Sean
Roe, Richard
Rooney, Patrick
Ryder, John
Ryder, William

Schweppe, Frederick
Shanahan, Philip
Shelly, Denis
Shelly, Thomas
Sheppard, M.I.
Shiels, James
Simpson, Terence
Slater, Michael
Slater, Thomas
Slater, William
Slattery, James
Smyth, Michael
Somers, Daniel Charles
Stapleton, William James
Stokes, Dick
Sweeney, P. Emmet

Turner, John
Tyrrell, Andrew

Ui Dalaigh, Liam

Walker, J.
Walker, Michael
Walsh, John
Walsh, Patrick
Ward, George
Ward, Nicholas
Whelehan, Christopher
Williams, Henry J.
Williams, Peter

Magazine Fort

Boland, Patrick
Gilligan, Bob
Holohan, Patrick Hugh

Marié, Louis
Martin, Christopher
Martin, Eamon

Murphy, John
Ó Briain, Sean

O hUallachain, Gearoid
Parker, Bernard
Roche, Timothy

Marrowbone Lane

Adams, John

Bailey, Patrick J.
Bowman, Joseph
Breathnach, Seamus
Burke, Matthew
Butler, Con
Butler, James
Byrne, Alphonsus
Byrne, Christopher
Byrne, Frank
Byrne, James
Byrne, Kate
Byrne, Michael
Byrne, Michael
Byrne, Patrick
Byrne, Patrick

Canty (or Casty), Thomas
Clarke, Joseph
Clince, Maria (née Quigley)
Colbert, Con
Cooney O'Brien, Annie
Cooney, Lillie
Corcoran, Joseph (Bro Louis OFM)
Corrigan, James
Cosgrave, Philip
Cullen, John

Darcy, John
Dempsey, William

Downey, Joseph
Doyle, Christopher
Doyle, May (née Byrne)
Doyle, Thomas J.
Doyle, Thomas
Dunne, Dennis K.
Dunne, Patrick J.
Dwyer, Michael

Edwards, John

Farrelly, Rose (née Mullally)
Fitzpatrick, James
Foley, William

Greene, Josephine (née Kelly)
Grehan, James

Harbourne, Eileen Cooney
Harbourne, Patrick
Harbourne, Sean
Harman, Patrick
Harmon, Brigid (née Hegarty)
Hendley, Emily (née O'Keeffe)
Holland, Daniel
Holland, Robert
Holland, Walter

Judge, John Patrick

Kavanagh, James
Kavanagh, Martin
Kavanagh, Priscilla (née
    Quigley)
Kelly, William
Kennedy, Joseph P.
Kennedy, Margaret
Kenny, James
Kenny, Kieran
Keogh, John
Kerrigan, Owen
Keys, John

Lamb, Patrick
Leigh, James
Liston, Michael
Lynch, Sighle (née
    O'Hanlon)

McCabe, Edward
McCabe, Michael B.
McCabe, Peter
McCabe, William
McCarthy, Patrick
MacDiarmuid, Lughaidh
McEvoy, Christopher
McGavan, Josephine
McGrath, Joseph
McGrath, Patrick
McGrath, Patrick
McGrath, Sean
McKenna, Bernard
McNamara, Rose
McNamee, Agnes
MacNeill, Diarmuid
Marrinan, Edward
Mason, D.H.

Morgan, John
Mullen, Martin
Mullen, Patrick
Murphy, Francis
Murphy, Kathleen
Murphy, Seamus
Murphy, Thomas
Murray, Gabriel B.
Murray, Harry S.

Nolan, George

O'Brennan, Lily M.
O Briain, Donncada
O'Brien, Patrick
O'Brien, Laurence
O'Brien, Peadar
O Broin, Padraig
O'Byrne, Hugh
O'Byrne, Sean
O'Caomhanaighe, Tomas
O'Carroll, Joseph
O'Connell, James
O Duinn, Peadar
O'Gorman, John J.
O'Gorman, Joseph
O'Hagan, James
O'Hanlon, Mollie
O'Neill, Edward
O'Neill, Jos
O'Neill, Michael
O'Riordan, Michael
O'Rourke, Patrick
O'Toole, John

Pairceir, Seosamh
Pender, Henry

Power, Arthur
Power, Joseph
Power, Liam

Roche, William

Saul, John
Simmons, Mgt (née
    O'Flaherty)
Spicer, Josephine

Teehan, James

Troy, Daniel
Troy, Patrick

Venables, Thomas

Walsh, James
Walsh, Patrick
White, Michael

Young, E.C.
Young, Patrick J.
Young, Robert
Young, Thomas

Mendicity Institute

Balfe, Richard C.
Brennan, James J.
Brooks, Fred

Clarke, John
Coleman, Richard
Crenigan, James
Cullen, John Francis

de Roiste, E.

Harrington, Sean
Heuston, Sean

Levins, George

Marks, James

Meehan, William

Norton, Joseph

O Broin, Seosamh S.
O Ceallaigh, Padraig
O'Dea, William,

Peppard, T.

Staines, Liam
Stephenson, P.J.

Wilson, James
Wilson, Peter
Wilson, Peter
Wilson, William

Roe's Distillery

Bowles, William P.
Byrne, George
Cunningham, Michael
Dowling Sean
Egan, Patrick
Fagan, William

Gaskin, Henry
Gogan, John Gerard
Haran, D.
Keely, Sean
Keogh, Martin
Nugent, John

O'Grady, Charles
O Murchadha, Seamus
Quinn, George J.

Ward, Bernard
Ward, Patrick J.
Ward Patrick

St Stephen's Green

Adams, John
Alexander, Nicholas

Brougham, James
Burke, Edward
Byrne, Christopher
Byrne, James
Byrne, Joseph

Carton, Owen
Clarke, Philip
Clifford, Tom
Conroy, Eileen
Conroy, Sean
Corcoran, James
Courtney, Bernard
Craven, Barney
Crothers, Christopher

Daniels, Harry
de Coeur, Robert
Donnelly, Michael
Doyle, Dennis
Doyle, Joseph
Duffy, Patrick
Dynan, Christopher

ffrench Mullen, Madeleine
Fitzmaurice Gerard
Fox, James
Fox, James
Foy, Martin

Fullerton, George

Geraghty, Eugene
Gifford, Helen (née
    Donnelly)
Goff, Bridget

Hackett, Rosie
Halpin, William
Hampton, James
Henry, Fred
Holden, Patrick J.
Hyland, May

Jackson, Peter
Joyce, James
Joyce, Mrs Maggie

Keenan, Thomas
Kelly, —
Kelly, Annie
Kelly, James
Keogh, James
King, Martin

Lambert, J.
Lawlor, Patrick J.
Leddy, Peter
Little, James
Luke (or Juke), Edward

McArt, Daniel
McCormick, Richard

The College of Surgeons, St. Stephen's Green

McDonald, John
MacGrath, Peter P.
Maguire, James
MacMahon, J.
Mahon, John
Mallin, Michael
Mannering, E.
Markievicz, Madam
Monks, Andrew
Moore, May (née Wisely)
Murphy, Fred
Murray, Daniel

Nicholls, Harry
Ni Dhubhgaill, Christine
   Maire

O Briain, Liam
O Briain, Liam
O'Brien, Frank

O'Daly, Nora
O'Daly, Mrs Bridget (née
   Murtagh)
O'Doherty, Michael
O'Kelly, Michael
O'Leary, David
O'Neill, John
O'Neill, Tim (Jim)
O'Reilly, Joseph
O'Reilly, Patrick
O'Shea, Robert

Partridge, William

Reynolds, Percy
Robbins, Frank
Ryan, Frederick
Ryan, Margaret
Shannon, Martin
Skinnider, Margaret

South Dublin Union

Arnold, James

Boylan, Thomas J.
Brugha, Cathal
Burke, Frank
Burke, James J.
Byrne, Joseph P.
Byrne, Liam

Carroll, Leo
Ceannt, Eamonn
Coady, William
Condron, William
Cosgrave, W.T.
Cullen, Thomas

Donnellan, Brendan
Downey, John
Doyle, Gerald
Doyle, Peadar

Evans, Robert J.

Farrell, Michael
ffrench Mullen, Douglas
Foran, James

Gibson, Edward
Gibson, Michael
Glynn, James

Irvine, George

Joyce, John V.

Keegan, Edward
Kelly, Joseph F.
Kenny, James
Kerr, Michael

MacCarthy, Dan
McDowell, William
McGlynn, Sean
McKenna, John
McMahon, Daniel J.
Maguire, James
Moloney, Patrick
Morrissey, James
Morrissey, Patrick S.
Murphy, John

O'Brien, Denis
O'Brien, Liam
O'Brien, Stephen L.
O'Corrigan, William
O'Doherty, John J.
O'Loughlin, Patrick
O Florbheartaigh, Liam
O Florbheartaigh, Seamus
O'Reilly, Patrick
O'Reilly, Richard
O'Shaughnessy, Sean
Owens, Sean

Quinn, James

Rigney, Paddy
Russell, James

Sears, David
Sweeney, Michael

Tracey, Sean
Traynor, Sean

Ward, Peter
Whelan, Richard.

In the original military plans for the Rising, Joseph Plunkett, Directory of Military Operations, prescribed 3,000 personnel as a minimum requirement. However, the Easter Monday muster of Volunteers was reduced to about half that number as a result of the confusion caused by the countermand. Of the 1,000 thousand members of the 4th Battalion commanded by Eamonn Ceannt, only about 90 answered reported at Emerald Square, though this number later increased to about 200. Accordingly plans for the Rising in Dublin had to be radically altered (see the map on pages 22 and 23.

Very few of the provincial Volunteer units participated in the Rising as combatants. The sequence of orders and counterorders led to inaction in Cork, Kerry, Limerick, and other areas in the south-west. Only Galway (OC Liam Mellowes) and Wexford (OC Robert Brennan) played an active role.

The List of Honour in the National Museum includes the provincial participants.

Mobilisation Order, April 1916

8 Easter 1917

In the period following the Rising political activities in Dublin and throughout the country were sternly discouraged and repressed by the British Government and the military and police. The first anniversary of the Rising was felt by many people to be a suitable occasion to demonstrate in commemoration of the dead patriots and their cause. A gesture to revive the spirit of the men of 1916 was suggested and acted upon by a small group of women attached to the Citizen Army. Their plan was to print and post up the Proclamation again upon all public buildings and vantage points and fly the tricolour flag of the Irish Republic from all buildings in Dublin associated with the Rising.

It was decided that the reissue of the Proclamation should bear more than a close resemblance to the original, so such type as had remained in the printing workshop at Liberty Hall was collected and handed to the printers. Thus it was that the original fount of type was used again.

The women arranged with Mr Joseph Stanley (who had printed the *Irish War News*) and his two employees, Mr Walker and his son Frank, to do the printing. To fulfil their promise of carrying out the work in time to allow for its distribution and posting-up by Easter, the men had to work through the whole of Good Friday night and part of Easter Saturday.

The reissue (for that is what it was; it was not a

facsimile copy of the original) is a very creditable imitation of the original. The paper used was of a different and better texture and colour than the original 1916 issue. A few typographical errors, notably the inverted 'e' in 'the' in the last paragraph of the original, were corrected.

The size is slightly larger – 514 × 768 mm, as compared with 508 × 762 mm, and the type area smaller – 707 × 448 mm as compared with 736 × 463 mm.

Of the innumerable reprints, copies and facsimiles, this 1917 reissue is the only one that may be regarded as of historical interest – in fact it is a bibliographical rarity as only one copy is known to exist.

The Starry Plough, flag of the Irish Citizen Army

The Proclamation Signatories

Padraig Henry Pearse

Born 10 November 1879 at 27 Great Brunswick Street, Dublin, he was the first-born child of James, a monumental sculptor from Devon, and Margaret Brady. As a child, an elderly aunt interested him in Irish history and he began to study Irish. He went to the Royal University (now University College, Dublin) and took a Barrister at Law degree though he never practised. Instead he became chief editor of *An Claidheamh Soluis,* official organ of the Gaelic League, and founded St Edna's College at Cullenswood House, Rathmines. He joined the Volunteers and made a memorable speech at the graveside of O'Donovan Rossa.

As Commander-in-Chief of the Volunteers he fought in the GPO. After the surrender he was tried on 2 May and executed on 3 May.

Thomas J. Clarke

Thomas Clark, of Leitrim and Tipperary parentage, was born on the Isle of Wight on 11 March 1857. His father served in the British Army and on retirement the family settled in Dungannon, a town of strong republican sympathies. At the age of twenty-one, Thomas was sworn into the Irish Republican Brotherhood. He went to the United States in 1880, became involved with Clan na Gael and was sent back to England to carry out an explosives campaign. This led to a sentence of life imprisonment in 1883; he served fifteen and a half years. Afterwards he returned to the US where he married Kathleen Daly, niece of the Fenian John Daly and sister of Ned Daly; the best man was Major John MacBride. They returned to Dublin in 1907 and set up a tobacconist and newsagency shop at 75A Parnell Street. He helped to reorganise the IRB and was one of the chief planners of the Rising. He was executed on 3 May 1916.

James Connolly

James Connolly was born on 5 June 1868 in Edinburgh of Irish parents, John, a farm labourer, and his wife Mary McGinn from County Monaghan. The family were very poor and James went to work at the age of eleven. Self educated, he became interested in Irish history and the problems of workers. On marriage to Lily Reynolds, they decided to return to Ireland where he founded the Irish Socialist Republican party and published a newspaper, the *Workers' Republic*. Objectives: Irish freedom and justice for workers. He settled briefly in the US, then returned to Ireland where he met James Larkin and became organiser for the newly established Irish Transport and General Workers' Union. The lock-out of 1913 led to the formation of the Irish Citizen Army in October 1913 and to participation in the Rising. He was executed on 12 May 1916.

Thomas MacDonagh

Thomas MacDonagh was born in Cloughjordan, County Tipperary, in 1878. He became a teacher, like his parents, and was caught up in the enthusiasm for the Irish language then sweeping the country. He went to the Aran Islands, joined Pearse at St Enda's in 1908, and became a Volunteer. Centre of a literary circle that included James Stephens. Padraic Colum and AE, he wrote poetry, a book on Thomas Campion and another on Irish literature. He was married to Muriel Gifford, sister of Joseph Plunkett's wife. In Easter Week, with his brother John, he fought in Jacob's. He was executed on 3 May.

Sean MacDiarmada

Sean MacDiarmada was born in Kiltyclogher, County Leitrim, in 1884, the son of a small farmer. He worked in Glasgow and Belfast before returning to Dublin where he met Thomas Clarke and was appointed national organiser of the

IRB in 1908. Two years later he was involved in setting up the republican paper *Irish Freedom*. Later he became a member of the Military Council that planned the Rising. He fought in the GPO and was executed on 12 May.

Eamonn Ceannt

Eamonn Ceant's father was from Tipperary, his mother from Galway, and there, at Glenamaddy, he was born on 21 September 1881. The family moved to Dublin where, later, the commemoration of the 1798 Rebellion woke his nationalist sympathies; he joined the Gaelic League and studied Irish. When he got a job in Dublin Corporation and married Aine O'Brennan, he seemed destined to a humdrum life, but the formation of the Volunteers in 1913 changed all that. He joined the Fourth Battalion and during the Rising his assignment was to hold the South Dublin Union with a small force of no more than ninety men. This he successfully did. He was executed on 8 May.

Joseph Plunkett

Joseph Mary Plunkett, youngest of the signatories, son of Count George Noble Plunkett of the family to which Saint Oliver Plunkett had belonged, was born in Dublin in 1887. Delicate in health, he suffered from TB and travelled a great deal, mainly to escape the damp of Ireland. In 1911 he met Thomas MacDonagh with whom he had much in common, particularly literature and the theatre. He became a contributor to *Irish Freedom* and was entrusted with a number of foreign missions on behalf of the Volunteer cause. He went to Germany to see Casement, to the US to contact John Devoy and Clan na Gael. Already seriously ill, he was picked out as a ringleader after the Rising, and condemned to death. One of the most poignant episodes of those historic days was his marriage to Grace Gifford on 3 May in Kilmainham Gaol. After the ceremony the lovers were immediately parted; he was executed the following morning.

Notes

The Cuchulainn Statue

Like Yeats, Pearse and other artists and writers, the sculptor Oliver Sheppard (1865–1941) was inspired by the image of the boy hero, Cuchulainn. Though a mythical character, he came to embody the ideals of patriotic courage and self-sacrifice.

Sheppard modelled the statue, which depicts the death of Cuchulainn, in 1911–2 and exhibited it for the first time in 1914. The plaster cast lay in his studio for many years until it was selected by the then Taoiseach, Eamon de Valera, as a memorial to the 1916 Rising. It was cast in bronze in Belgium and installed in the GPO in 1935.

Sheppard was instructor in modelling at the Dublin Metropolitan School of Arts from 1902; one of his pupils was Willie Pearse, younger brother of Padraig.

Kilmainham Gaol

On the west side of Dublin city, Kilmainham Gaol was built in 1796 on a slope towards the little valley of the River Camac known as Gallows Hill. The rear walls which rise from this valley are almost 80 feet high. The main entrance is set within two curving walls of limestone, 600 feet in circumference, over one-third of a mile in length and four feet thick.

Since the Rebellion of 1798 and until its closure in 1924, many of the most notable figures in Irish history have passed through its gates. Its transformation from gaol to museum was due to the dedicated efforts of the Kilmainham Restoration Committee, set up in the 1930s on the initiative of Sean Dowling, who was a kinsman of Padraig Pearse, and Patrick O'Connor, librarian in the National Library and a veteran of 1916.

Index

Figures underlined indicate photographs

JOHN O'CONNOR was born in Killorglin, County Kerry. He was a member of the staff of the National Library of Ireland for a number of years where he specialised in historical research. Later he took up appointment in the public service when he regularly represented Ireland at international meetings. He was a member of the inaugural Kilmainham Restoration Committee.

He is the author of *The Workhouses of Ireland*.